D1046927

HIGHWIRE

MANAGEMENT

GENE
CALVERT

HIGHWIRE MANAGEMENT

RISK-TAKING TACTICS FOR LEADERS, INNOVATORS, AND TRAILBLAZERS

Jossey-Bass Publishers · San Francisco

Copyright © 1993 by Jossey-Bass Inc., Publishers, 350 Sansome Street,
San Francisco, California 94104. Copyright under International, Pan
American, and Universal Copyright Conventions. All rights reserved.
No part of this book may be reproduced in any form—except for brief
quotation (not to exceed 1,000 words) in a review or professional
work—without permission in writing from the publishers.

Substantial discounts on bulk quantities of Jossey-Bass books
are available to corporations, professional associations, and other
organizations. For details and discount information, contact the
special sales department at Jossey-Bass Inc., Publishers.
(415) 433-1740; Fax (415) 433-0499.

For sales outside the United States, contact Maxwell Macmillan
International Publishing Group, 866 Third Avenue, New York,
New York 10022.

Manufactured in the United States of America

 The paper used in this book is acid-free and meets the
State of California requirements for recycled paper
(50 percent recycled waste, including 10 percent
postconsumer waste), which are the strictest guidelines
for recycled paper currently in use in the United States.

10% POST
CONSUMER
WASTE

Library of Congress Cataloging-in-Publication Data

Calvert, Gene, date.
    Highwire management : risk-taking tactics for leaders, innovators,
and trailblazers / Gene Calvert. — 1st ed.
        p.   cm. — (Jossey-Bass management series)
    Includes bibliographical references and index.
    ISBN 1-55542-553-4 (acid-free paper)
    1. Risk management.   2. Decision-making   3. Risk management—
United States—Case studies.   I. Title.   II. Series.
HD61.C35   1993
658.4—dc20   93-5385
                                                                  CIP

Credits are on page 225.

FIRST EDITION
HB Printing   10 9 8 7 6 5 4 3 2 1   *Code 9373*

*The Jossey-Bass
Management Series*

Contents

Preface

Traditional guidelines for management risk taking do not meet the critical challenges that will ensure business survival into the twenty-first century. Like it or not, risk taking is a vital component of these status quo–shattering challenges: *managing productivity* with reduced resources, shorter cycles, and increased workloads; *managing morale* in flattened or downsized organizations; *managing profits* in recessionary or slow-growth economic periods; *managing competitiveness* in new, niche-driven, or global markets; *managing change,* from quality improvements to technology innovations, maintaining stability in day-to-day matters; *managing the performance of knowledge workers,* the single greatest asset and bottom-line leverage point in any organization today; and *managing followership* in an era of widespread mistrust, fear, and cynicism.

These and other crucial challenges alter and accelerate management risk taking drastically and indefinitely. Nothing protects you from them and from the risk dilemmas they impose—not the size of your organization, the soundness of your strategy, or the success of your career. The increased necessity and importance of risk taking to survive and succeed today raises the following difficult questions for you as a manager:

- Why should I take a risk when I'm expected to avoid risk taking?

- When does it make sense to initiate management programs with uncertain outcomes in order to achieve high-gain goals?

- Will my career survive if my risks fail?

- How do I motivate myself and others to initiate risks and then take action responsibly?

- How can I make risk taking a more positive experience?

Highwire Management addresses these questions by outlining and explaining the tools and tactics necessary for handling management risks effectively. It is both a sourcebook and a tactical manual, designed to help you approach risks in a responsible way so that you can aim for—and ultimately attain—ever higher levels of excellence.

Three views of risk taking undergird *Highwire Management:* risking as a *management practice,* which refers to the nuts and bolts of decision making and implementation; risking as *management philosophy,* referring to the core set of principles that drive risk-taking assumptions and actions; and risking as a *management strategy,* meaning the vision, plan, and methods for achieving organizational or divisional goals. The integration of these three perspectives supports effective, growth-oriented management in today's increasingly demanding and often chaotic business environment.

Who Should Read This Book?

Managers at all levels of experience and responsibility face the prospect of taking more frequent risks—and larger risks as well. The tactics presented in *Highwire Management* will help you meet that challenge, whatever your management orientation, organizational setting, level of employment, or field of activity. You may wish to foster selective risk taking among associates or you might want to encourage innovation and entrepreneurship. Your organizational environment may be conservative and regimented, or it might be volatile and chaotic. Regardless of your background, experience, or inclination, if you aspire to excel as a manager, you need to develop the agility to cross the risk highwire.

Approaching the Highwire

Being able to maintain balance on the management highwire requires training and practice. *Highwire Management* emphasizes a number of approaches to sharpen your risk expertise and help you acquire the agility to walk the highwire with confidence. They include

- *Expanding your risk resources. Highwire Management* furnishes you with a vast array of experience-based and research-based management risk tactics. However vast your inventory of tactics may be, you will find additional ones in this book.

- *Challenging your risk attitudes.* Expect to have many of your risk-taking assumptions challenged, especially your negative views of risk. Whether you view management risk taking in a positive or negative light, be prepared to reconsider that view.

- *Updating your risk expertise.* The recent surge in research and writing related to management risking has added much to our practical understanding. *Highwire Management* summarizes and examines the most up-to-date information.

- *Assessing your risk skills.* The self-assessment tools in *Highwire Management* measure your risk-taking beliefs and behavior and help you set priorities in developing your skills and strategies.

Learning from the experiences of others is key to your own risk-taking success. In *Highwire Management* you will also read about the actual risk experiences of managers from a variety of backgrounds and benefit from the advice they offer on risk-taking tactics.

Overview of the Contents

Part One of *Highwire Management* looks at how managers respond to risk and uncertainty. Chapter One examines the new set of rules required for riding the turbulent rapids of economic and social change and explains why a more risk-filled business environment requires more risk-oriented management skills and strategies. Chapter Two counters the negative image of risk taking with an exploration of its many worthwhile and overlooked rewards. When managers see the payoffs, they begin to recognize the value of risk taking for their work, careers, and organizations.

Part Two presents skill-building tactics for handling risks. Chapter Three provides tools to assess your risk-taking history as a manager. Taking an inventory of your strengths and weaknesses will build a foundation for developing your risk-taking skills.

There is a tendency among managers to view the decision-making process differently when it involves risks. Chapter Four reveals the subtle ways that a distorted perspective can undermine your managerial effectiveness.

Although research and statistics are essential components of the risk-taking process, raw data will never provide all the answers. In Chapter Five, you will find suggestions for avoiding "data addiction" and for using intuition as a balancing factor in high-quality analysis.

Chapter Six delves into the intense emotional undercurrents that run through the risk-taking process. Preparing for them is one of the prerequisites of confident risk taking. Making timely and well-informed decisions is the key, and managing emotional reflexes is the doorway to success.

Chapter Seven discusses the hidden costs that can tip the balance of your risk-taking venture. Investing in expert advice, for example, can reduce potential hazards, but without proper management, the costs can escalate and the tactic can backfire.

Whether you take major management risks once a year or once a day, knowing how to survive the failures will allow you to continue risking in an environment that demands it. Chapter Eight points out the value of converting failure into learning.

In Part Three I focus on how to nurture your own skills and foster risk taking in others. Chapter Nine emphasizes the importance of learning through action, with the goal of cultivating your risk taking through conscious and ongoing effort. The need to foster responsible risk taking in associates is the subject of Chapter Ten. New ways to use incentive plans and build trust are among the recommended methods for meeting that need.

There is no longer any doubt that the new business environment demands new rules of risk taking. The enormous challenges confronting us as we near the new century suggest the need for a reexamination and re-working of our risk assumptions and methods of oper-ation. It is a precondition for survival on the high-risk highwire and a vital first step in preparing for a future that belongs to those willing to risk.

Washington, D.C.   GENE CALVERT
July 1993

Acknowledgments

Readers may wonder why authors feel the need to thank so many people. I have learned it takes more people to produce a publishable book than could ever be imagined. Crediting them by name is the least I can do to show appreciation for their generous gifts of advice, expertise, and feedback.

For their detailed comments on nearly every page of the draft manuscript, I heartily thank Lisa Marshall, Sandra Mobley, and Bill O'Rourke. For offering their immensely helpful reactions to portions of the manuscript, I also thank Lori Annaheim, Keith Blurton, Joan Cassidy, Lowell Christy, Edyie DeVincenci, Antonia Fitzgerald, Kay Heillig, Gary LaBranche, Suzanne Lulewicz, Leeda P. Marting, Thomas Morris III, Deborah Perry, Bruce Ritter, Bill Roth, Janet Stevens, Michael Thomas, Joelyn Watson, and Burke Wilkenson. For in-depth, constructive feedback on the final draft, I thank reviewers Amy Edmondson, Gordon Pitz, and Alan Rowe and Jossey-Bass employees Marcella Friel, Patricia O'Hare, and Terri Welch.

Several people were most helpful in arranging research interviews: Briana Beeby, Greg Freeman, Sharon

Hadary, and Milt Mitler. There are many others to whom I am grateful for the special ways they supported me in the writing of this book: Tom Allen for his "getting published" course and book proposal advice; Ray Bard for believing in a first-time author as well as for guiding me through the find-a-publisher phase as my agent; Tom Harris for suggesting the title for the book and for his constant support of this venture; Sallie Holder for typing and administrative help; Graham Keene for prodding me to practice my risk rhetoric; Judy Katzel for superb editing at the start; Gail Lehmann for persuading clients to invest in my risk-taking seminars, where I tested many of the ideas in *Highwire Management;* Paul Lukacs for manuscript typing, proofing, and permissions assistance; Kathleen Ryan for advising and supporting me at several discouraging impasses; Charlotte Taylor for discussing the concept of this book with me many years ago; and Rosalie Woods for her persistent editorial improvements in the second and third drafts. I also thank the brave people listed in the Appendix, who were willing to speak out in print about their risk-taking beliefs and experiences.

I also wish to thank the highly dedicated and competent professionals at Jossey-Bass, who helped so much to improve the book and make it available: Bill Hicks for seeing a publishable book amid the good intentions of a first draft and for then shaping it to realize his vision; Cedric Crocker for guiding me expertly through the review and rewriting process; Laura Simonds and her colleagues in sales and marketing; Marcella Friel and Mary Garrett for their savvy judgment and energetic work at the production phase; Tad Lathrop for his copyediting skills, insights, and logic; and Michael Martin for his creative direction of the book's jacket design and input on the internal design.

Finally, there are a few people I wish to thank here

for strictly personal reasons: Charles Marshal Calvert, Mary Darlene Lindsay, Ron Willis, and Helene Zeitlin. And for anyone my fallible memory overlooked, I beg his or her gentle forgiveness.

G.C.

*To my wife, Christine Nykiel Calvert,
the shining, pure, and enduring
miracle of my life*

The Author

GENE CALVERT is a management trainer, consultant, and speaker for organizations of all sizes and types. During his twenty-year career he has managed educational programs in technology, health, and professional development fields. He has also presented management programs in Central America, the Caribbean, and England. He is a faculty member of the Institutes for Organization Management of the U.S. Chamber of Commerce, as well as adjunct associate professor of management at the University of Maryland and Johns Hopkins University.

Calvert has appeared on network television, national satellite broadcasts, and cable programs to discuss his views on management issues. He was interviewed by the National Association of Independent Businesses for a syndicated radio series aimed at small businesses.

Calvert earned his M.P.H. degree in public health from Harvard University and his Ph.D. degree in sociology from Case Western Reserve University.

HIGHWIRE

MANAGEMENT

PART ONE

The Value of Risk Taking

1

THE NEW REALITIES: WALKING THE MANAGEMENT HIGHWIRE

Closing the gap between old management rules and the new realities of competing in the twenty-first century has become a growing problem for managers. Practicing a balanced approach to management risk taking can help solve the problem. That essential practice will require pragmatic risk-taking tactics and skills—the "right stuff" in a management world increasingly characterized by unpredictability.

THE NEW RULES

The changing business environment requires a revision of established risk-taking expectations and methods. Traditionally, managers were supposed to be risk averse to the extreme. Today they still need to avoid management risks that are unnecessary, unwise, and unrewarding. At the same time, however, they must begin to loosen their rigid adherence to an ethos based on risk aversion. They need to more favorably consider the opportunities created by chaotic changes that justify a greater number of responsible risks than in the past. This means accepting the fact that the new, perpetually uncertain environment requires greater management risk taking. And they need to recognize the changes that justify taking a greater number of responsible risks than in the past.

Risk taking has long been considered an irresponsible management practice. It has not been viewed as a legitimate, necessary function of business leadership. But now, management risk taking must be viewed in a more positive and appreciative light. Risk takers, in fact, are increasingly being seen as effective agents of change. "Show me an innovator, and I'll show you a risk taker," says the president of the U.S. Chamber of Commerce, Richard Lesher (1992).

Managers at all levels of authority and responsibility must revise their conservative risk-taking attitudes and practices. They must see risk as an everyday tactic, not just an occasional strategy. They also have to recognize that the ability to manage risks is a learned and acquired skill, not simply an inborn personality trait.

Managers need a new set of risk-taking rules suited to the new realities of managing in an unpredictable, uncertain, and unforgiving business environment—an environment that demands a greater sense of pragmatism and realism than ever before. The skill with which managers apply these new rules will determine how well they perform on the highwire of management risk taking.

When you as a manager take risks, your aim is a higher level of management performance. You reach for greater achievement, testing your managerial judgment and conviction. You step forward in pursuit of a higher but riskier summit of peak management and organizational performance. It is like choosing to play for larger stakes on a tougher playing field. High-gain risk taking challenges you to back your management vision with your managerial actions.

Risk takers know that "staying the same can lose

the game" in management and business today. They also believe that risk taking is playing the game to win. Not risking is playing the game to break even at best.

If you want to be an average manager or have an average organization, little risk taking is required. But if you set ambitious goals as an individual, team, or organization, then high-gain/high-loss risk taking will be required. And that demands that you walk on the highwire of management risk taking.

KNOWING THE RISK HIGHWIRE

A broader and deeper understanding of the risk highwire will serve you in several ways. It will enable you to anticipate and spot risks and will make it easier to distinguish and analyze core risk elements. It will help you to develop strategies for undertaking specific risks. Ultimately, it will prepare you to decide when and when not to venture forth.

In a state of risk, four essential factors come into play: uncertainty, loss, gain, and significance.

Uncertainty is simply the unpredictability of outcomes, some less desirable than others. One example might be an increase versus a decrease in decision-making speed as a consequence of expanding the authority of middle managers. Some experts see risk and uncertainty as the essentially same thing. Others argue that risks have clear probabilities and that uncertainty lacks them (Bazerman, 1986). What matters is expecting uncertain possibilities in every management risk, regardless of what can be known about the probability of their actually happening.

A loss is simply a decrease in the value of something, such as a decline in professional reputation or a reduction in stock price. Without the possibility of loss, there is no true risk.

Gains are the most desired outcome of any risk, such as enhancing your professional reputation or increasing your stock price.

What drives managers' interest in risk the most, however, is the significance of the gains and losses. Significance is how much a risk outcome matters to those for whom it counts the most. A loss of market share for product line A will matter a lot to those selling it; it will matter little to those selling product line B, unless of course, they are connected in some way, as with the chips used by computer manufacturers.

Risking is experimenting to find out how good any person, organization, or thing can be. It is driving in the fast lane of the economic freeway. It is stepping nervously but bravely into the unknown for good reason. It is doing something totally new and unproven.

Viewed from this angle, risk is akin to progress and innovation. Such a close relationship suggests the most sensible reason to take risks: to achieve positive gains that enrich the status quo. The forward-moving nature of risk taking requires boldness in the face of unexpected and potentially detrimental consequences.

Taking risks is facing "some kind of peril, jeopardy, hazard, or exposure to the chance of injury or loss," as defined by the *Oxford English Dictionary*. It is "the potential for realization of unwanted, negative consequences of an event" (Rowe, 1977b, p. 24). By nature it entails the possibility of success or failure. Risk equals uncertainty plus potential for damage (Webber and Bottom, 1989).

Risking is making decisions that entail potentially negative consequences, under conditions of uncertainty. Risking as decision making also assumes another condition: choice of action. This means you have the twin options of trying to produce wanted outcomes, such as ensuring gains, as well as preventing unwanted outcomes, such as losses (Rescher, 1983). When you challenge sacred but outmoded management practices, you expose yourself to significant, if uncertain, negative consequences, such as resentment or retaliation, that could slow your upward career movement. As with any risk decision, however, you can initiate actions generating positive outcomes and blocking negative ones. It is in implementing risk decisions that you encounter their full force and effect most directly.

The new rules of risk taking apply to what experts call *speculative,* as opposed to *pure,* risks. *Pure risks* are unpredictable and involve only undesirable outcomes, like whether or not an employee is injured on the job. Insurance is purchased to cover pure risks. *Speculative risks,* or management risks, are different. They are uninsurable, and they lead directly to one of three outcomes: a loss, no change, or a gain. Figure 1.1 illustrates the difference between pure and speculative risks.

While speculative risks may have some degree of predictability, they still cause discomfort for most deci-

Figure 1.1. Risk Outcomes.

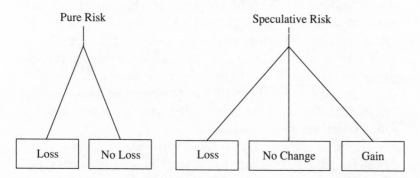

Source: Athearn, Pritchett, and Schmit, 1989, p. 3. Used by permission.

sion makers. This discomfort stems from the inability to know confidently enough—or to calculate precisely enough—the relevant uncertainties in speculative risks. The new rules task managers with expanding both their psychological tolerance of these uncertainties and their actions to anticipate and to mitigate them.

Uncertainty is a subjective and normally unpleasant state of mind. Managers are seldom fully aware of the magnitude of a risk, and their natural inclination is to reduce the level of uncertainty. How a manager handles that instinctive need determines whether he or she becomes a risk taker or a risk avoider. For example, risk avoiders, as Figure 1.2 shows, react more subjectively and negatively to uncertainty than do risk takers. Risk avoiders prefer to handle uncertainty by either actively or passively avoiding the risk and the unacceptable uncertainty it imposes entirely.

THE EXPERIENCE
OF RISKING

For most managers, hiring and promotion decisions always involve significant elements of risk. Consider the costs to you and the organization if your assessment of an employee's performance proves inadequate. In a sense, then, risk hovers ghostlike above every management decision, however mundane or unusual. Yet the most intense awareness of the presence of risk occurs when you decide to do something you have not yet attempted or accomplished.

Risk is inherently a trial-and-error process. The blunders and miscalculations, as well as the successes, identify themselves only afterward. Every management risk that is taken or avoided sets off a chain reaction in which various forces collide explosively. Each manage-

Figure 1.2. Risk-Averse Behavior.

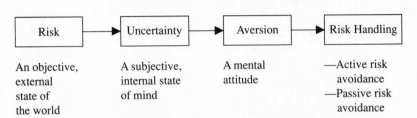

Risk	Uncertainty	Aversion	Risk Handling
An objective, external state of the world	A subjective, internal state of mind	A mental attitude	—Active risk avoidance —Passive risk avoidance

Source: Adapted from Athearn, Pritchett, and Schmit, 1989, p. 7. Used by permission.

ment risk involves a mix of elements that have never existed before in exactly the same sequence or combination. The process of developing new products, for example, may be standardized, but no single product travels through the process in exactly the same way, even with the same team of people.

You risk whether or not you act. Should you, for example, assume the risks of action by opposing a questionable, but widely supported, project involving your unit? Or should you invite the risks of inaction by remaining silent and going along with the will of the majority? Either could hurt or help you and your unit. Speaking out could make enemies and threaten the project's success. Staying mum could damage your reputation and self-respect or allow limited resources to be squandered on an ill-advised project.

Any serious and consequence-laden risk puts managers in a decision-making quandary: whether to act or not to act—whether to passively accept the uncertain outcomes of not risking or to actively initiate uncertain outcomes. Like business-suited performers in the "To be or not to be" scene from Shakespeare's *Hamlet,* managers ponder their equally consequential alternatives. One might imagine a particularly reflective manager updating Hamlet's famous soliloquy:

To risk, or not to risk, that is the question:
Whether 'tis smarter in the end to suffer
The slings and arrows of the status quo,
Or to take arms against a sea of uncertainty,
And by risking, achieve extraordinary goals.
To risk, to fail—
And by failing to say we end
The headaches and thousand stressful shocks
That managers are heir to. To risk, to fail—
Perchance to be humiliated—ay, there's the rub,
For in risk failure what retributions may come,
When we have lost our prominence, promotion, or
     pay,
Must give us ulcers; there's the quandary
That causes calamity for management risk takers.
Thus management culture doth make risk avoiders
     of us all,
And this natural urge for innovation and growth
Is covered over with the pale cast of cynicism,
And enterprises of great profit and progress
With these fears their possibilities eliminate,
And lose the name of action.

RISK METAPHORS

Risk metaphors help to illustrate the deeply personal
and intense experience of risking. Metaphors enable one
to examine, by comparative example, sensations associated with taking risks. Consider which of the following
metaphors best expresses the way you experience risk
taking: walking a highwire, climbing mountain peaks, or
guiding tree logs along wild and roaring rivers.

Highwire Walking
Risking is like walking a thin tightrope high above the
ground without a safety net. Those afraid of heights may
find that this metaphor portrays their own dread of tak-

ing risks. Even managers unafraid of heights acknowledge their anxiety or uneasiness at having to negotiate
the highwire of risk one nerve-racking step at a time,
trying not to look down or lose their balance.

Managers approach the tightrope of risk taking in different ways. Some run from it; others run toward it. Some
inch across it; others dance across it. Some find the height
of the highwire unnerving, while others find it exhilarat-
ing. Some concentrate on not falling off; others freeze their
eyes on the platform of safety at the end of the wire. Some
are never even aware of crossing the risk highwire, while
others feel like they are on the risk highwire even though
they may be only a foot above solid ground.

When you closely examine this metaphor, you can
quickly identify some of the ways to cross management
highwires safely and successfully. Learn the size, length,
and condition of the highwire—that is, learn the scale,
time frame, and hazards of your risk. Check the current
wind conditions—that is, check the current organizational risk environment. Know the best footing, when to
freeze, and when to speed up while crossing the highwire—know how to plan and execute management risks.
Gradually raise the height of the highwire—allow yourself the time and experience to acquire the risk knowledge
and skill for increasingly high levels of management risk
taking. Develop a sense of balance and centering—learn
how to concentrate on your risk and take each step carefully. Maintain a reliable safety net—keep your risk-
failure safety net in superb condition at all times. In sum,
these tightrope metaphors underscore the need to become
an expert in every aspect of a risk before you take it.

Climbing Mountains
Risking is like climbing a treacherous mountain, one that
poses life-threatening dangers to even the most experienced climber. This metaphor brings to mind some of

the greatest risks managers face, like those that involve gambling with the job or the company. Only a skilled risk taker would try to climb the Mount Everest of risk. A real-life mountain climb by Stanford Business School faculty member Jim Collins (1990) brings to light some important risk-taking rules.

Jim and a less experienced partner were climbing a five-hundred-foot granite cliff in Colorado called Cynical Pinnacle, a climb rated "most difficult" by professional climbers. Jim and his partner met each challenge of Cynical Pinnacle until everything started going wrong. As often happens in a risky venture, Jim's partner became too exhausted to finish the final part of the climb.

No sooner had Jim finished the last fifty feet of the climb alone than a lightning storm hit, literally making his hair stand on end. The rain made the rock "slippery as hell." Time started running out, with only two to three hours of daylight left. The temperature dropped quickly, numbing and stiffening Jim's muscles.

The situation worsened during the descent, when Jim's partner did not rappel down the cliff correctly and forgot to check whether a rope knot was clear of a crack in the wall. Jim's partner missed the rope tossed up to him, and Jim was unable to catch it as it fell back down. The climbers were stranded on Cynical Pinnacle as it turned dark. They could not last until daylight by clinging with cold, numbed fingers to tiny crevices in a vertical wall of rock. In the end, Jim rescued his partner; he put his own life at risk while exhibiting superb emotional control and mental concentration.

Jim persuaded a rescue squad to let him climb up the rock again, despite their doubts about his ability to repeat the climb in an exhausted state. Despite extreme physical fatigue, Jim found a crack system in the wall. He reached his partner after an hour of feeling his way along the mist-shrouded wall. His partner's hands were too numb to hold the ropes, but Jim rigged them to rappel him down anyway. They both touched ground safely at about 3:00 a.m. Jim now climbs less dangerous mountains, in keeping with his reordered value system: staying alive for those he loves most.

Jim's nearly fatal mountain climb, when studied as a risk-taking metaphor, illustrates the harsh but priceless lessons to be learned from even the worst risk-taking experience. The following rules are adaptable to climbing management mountains:

- Even the most precisely planned risk venture can whirl out of control as a result of unforeseen forces.
- Even the luckiest risk taker eventually experiences misfortune.
- You find the true limits of risk taking by exceeding and then somehow surviving them.
- Each additional member of the risk-taking team increases the chances of both risk success and failure.
- Risk-taking failure can reorder your value system in positive ways.
- You can pursue scaled-down risks and still relish your risk taking.
- It is dangerous to overestimate your margin of survivable risk error.
- Invest in more than one backup plan.
- Your ability to respond calmly and creatively can save you from risk-taking disaster.

Driving River Logs

At the turn of this century, the only way huge logs could be transported from remote and inaccessible mountain forests was along rivers unsuitable for lumber schooners or rafting. A tough breed of "river drivers" steered hurling, pitching, and rolling tree logs down swollen springtime rivers to lumber mills by standing astride them. "[River drivers] put order in the watery wildness as it swept them on" (Cox, 1947, p. 38). When logs collided into snags and pileups, the drivers would leap from one moving log to another, facing and eluding injury or death with each quick movement. Besides balletic agility, river drivers need skill in making life-and-death decisions on a moment-to-moment basis. Naturally, serious injuries and fatalities were commonplace. The dangers were compounded by the need to work feverishly to float the logs downstream while the river levels were temporarily raised by the melting snow.

Some of the same skills needed by river drivers apply to management risk taking—for example, extraordinary quickness, equilibrium, and instantaneous decision making (Pike, 1967). Management river drivers also navigate "hurtling, pitching and rolling" projects through twisting organizational rapids. And, again like river drivers, managers must know hundreds of small details and maneuvers to reach their goals unharmed.

ZONES OF MANAGEMENT RISKING

Whether you see yourself as a taker or avoider of risks, three realities haunt you every day as a manager. The first is the pervasiveness of management risk. It is a part of every decision you make or avoid, whether large or small. The second reality is the inevitability of management risk. Avoiding one only creates another set: the risks of not risking. The third reality is the cost of management risk. Such costs range from personal termination to organizational bankruptcy and everything in between.

These three realities lurk behind every management

decision you make. You confront them, for example, whenever you set business growth priorities, delegate critical tasks to subordinates, allocate funds among competing projects or units, develop new or change current products or services, or implement cost-cutting programs. Your ability to anticipate, assess, and handle such risks partly determines how far up the management ladder you climb, as well as whether your organization prospers or declines. The zones of risk taking—that is, common management risks—are shown in the list that follows. Consider the potential emotional and career ramifications of each item.

Type of Risk	*Selected Risk Options*
Technology risks	Buying or leasing any new technology
Financial risks	Increasing or decreasing debt load
Ethical risks	Blowing the whistle or keeping quiet
Human resource risks	Spending a lot or a little on training
Product/service risks	Creating new ones or changing current ones
Planning risks	Short-term versus long-term priorities
Organizational risks	Flattening or maintaining the pyramid
Strategic risks	Forming joint ventures or going it alone
Competitive risks	Leading or following in the industry
Career risks	Accepting or turning down an assignment
Marketing risks	Entering new markets or staying in current ones

Legal risks	Going to trial or settling out of court
Global risks	Expanding domestically or internationally

Collectively and synergistically, the many zones of management risk taking point to urgently needed shifts in management attitude and action: from opposition to support and from disparagement to appreciation. The more progressive and positive the view of voluntary management risk taking, the greater the chance of gains instead of just losses.

Many managers prefer to wait until a crisis forces them to take any but the most ordinary risks. A survey of twenty-two thousand manufacturing employees found that nearly two-thirds of them think before anything is done by management that a problem has to become a crisis (*Wall Street Journal*, 1989). While it is true that a crisis provokes risk taking like nothing else, the price is often high. Indeed, the Japanese vice minister of international affairs, Makoto Utsumi, stressed that because a crisis is a situation where things are out of control, it is too big to take on as a risk. It is a better policy to work with things that can be controlled (Sterngold, 1992). The lesson is clear: those who wait until a crisis forces them to take a risk place themselves in double jeopardy. They end up managing the risk and the crisis at the same time.

The vice president for worldwide purchasing at General Motors, J. Ignacio Lopez de Arriortura, understands instinctively the new rules of management of risk taking. Considered a prototype of the new manager at GM, Lopez is "a shirt-sleeve executive willing to get down in the trenches and take risks" (Brown and Swoboda, 1993, p. H-5). GM itself exemplifies the once stodgy corporation in a desperate race to survive by redesigning its management culture. It, too, is changing its risk-taking style, for example, by replacing managers of the company on the board of directors almost exclusively with outsiders—and by putting management risk takers like Lopez in charge of leading the changes.

A more risk-oriented manager like Lopez grasps clearly the need to find innovative, if uncertain, solutions to managing in today's environment. He even asks outside suppliers, who provide over half of GM's parts, to take big risks. He asks them to provide better-quality parts at lower prices in exchange for the promise of long-term contracts. According to Brown and Swoboda (1993), Lopez not surprisingly, believes this is tough and difficult work and attacks it with almost evangelical fervor: "This country is at the X [the crossroads]. With excuses, we will not be a great country. Do we want to quit or do we want to work hard?" Pacesetting managers like Lopez recognize the competitive realities and consequently the necessity to take risks.

General Electric, one of the most profitable and closely watched firms in America, embodies the changes ushering in new rules of risk taking for organizations and managers. As an organization, GE has reordered its priorities in acutely risk-charged ways, for example, through their focus on reducing bureaucratization and cutting across functional boundaries (Hyatt and Naj, 1992). However commonsensical the changes are in theory, implementing them raises significant issues—issues relevant to any organization competing in a global marketplace that more than one manager describes as "brutally Darwinian."

The well-publicized criteria used by CEO Jack Welch to promote GE managers also signify an upping of the risk-taking ante on a managerial level at GE. Managers are now expected, for example, to deliver on any commitment, to share company values, to make their numbers, and to inspire, not force, employee performance (Hyatt and Naj, 1992). When explicitly demanded and strictly enforced, as at GE, these criteria force managers to revise normal rules of risk taking. Consider, for instance, the greater risk taking entailed in making formal commitments and forecasts when you are expected to meet them nearly 100 percent, as at GE. Then consider the additional risks when the usual unexpected problems prevent or delay delivering on your projections.

As organizations escalate their standards of management performance, they implicitly change the rules of management risk taking. As organizations expect more and more from managers—in this and other ways—the need to revise and recognize new rules of risk taking becomes more and more urgent.

New risk-taking rules such as these help managers to set viable courses through an unpredictable, uncertain, and unforgiving business environment. They are essential aspects of performing on the highwire of management risk taking.

2

EXCELLENCE AND INNOVATION:
THE REWARDS OF RISK TAKING

> Uncertainty is an invitation to innovate, to
> create; uncertainty is the blank page in the au-
> thor's typewriter, the granite block before a
> sculptor, the capital in the hands of an investor,
> or the problem challenging the inventive mind of
> a scientist or an engineer. In short, uncertainty is
> the opportunity to make the world a better place.
> —Walter B. Wriston

Given their real dangers, why should you voluntarily
take management risks? The answer reveals one of the
least known secrets of risk mastery. In a nutshell, the
rewards of risking by choice can far outweigh the ultimate gains of doing so only when necessary.

If you dispute this notion, the majority of managers
will agree with you. They advocate caution as a nonnegotiable standard of managerial competence and a universal precondition of managerial success. They reduce
the number of their risk ventures, if at all possible. Some
go so far as to condemn optional and deliberate risk taking as a sign of managerial naiveté and ineptitude.

So again, the key question: Why should you walk
precariously on the risk highwire when you can stroll

safely on solid ground? This chapter begins the process of answering that question. It presents several defensible rationales for initiating risks as a manager and makes the case for the benefits of such action, thus restoring some balance to what has largely been a one-sided debate.

SURVIVING CHAOTIC TIMES

Managers now work in what London Business School professor Charles Handy calls the *Age of Unreason* (1990). It is a confusing, danger-plagued time when decisions are chancier and less controllable than ever before. No expected future is inevitable. The status quo no longer offers the best way forward. In sum, no predictions hold true. It is an age and a time, "therefore, for bold imaginings . . . for thinking the unlikely and doing the unreasonable," writes Handy (p. 5).

If, however, you agree that change is "another word for growth, another synonym for learning" (p. 5), such times present golden opportunities and lavish prizes to those willing to learn and grow, and that means taking elective management risks more often. The lion's share of rewards in an Age of Unreason flow to managers who pursue gains, as well as prevent losses, no matter how bleak or bewildering the times and to organizations who learn how to learn more quickly and efficiently, no matter how erratic the times.

Even if you doubt that chaotic times warrant "unreasonable" management tactics, there are specific forces at work in the management environment that are necessitating a movement toward taking risks.

- Pressure on managers to increase productivity with fewer people and less time and money

- Pressure on all managers—especially those at middle levels—to take action in order to survive personnel reductions, forced layoffs and "early outs," mergers, acquisitions, and so on

- Pressure on companies to make huge investments to remain competitive

- Pressure on senior managers to make organizational changes, such as radical restructurings that might include, for example, elimination of management layers

- Pressure on all individuals to shift careers, perhaps several times, just to survive

Constance Alexander, a former AT&T executive and now president of INTEX Communications, has, in a few key words, captured the essence of some of these disruptive changes (Murphy, Sperling, and Sperling, 1991, pp. 257–258):

The corporation,
you see,
is in the midst of
downsizing
resizing
right-sizing
redesigning
restructuring
reshaping
reapproximating
reorganizing
retrofitting
reshuffling the boxes
playing the blue chip version
of three card monte
sketching the new
infrastructure
on the back of a

cocktail napkin
so we can be
lean and mean,
Like assassins.
Wild dogs.
A marathon runner
with PMS.

The changes in the management environment pose greater dangers for those who are resistant to risk than for those who approach it with an open mind. In an unstable and unruly business world, the safest, most rewarding choice is to seek out, not run from, management risks. Disruptive changes create the need for managers to take more risks, to take smarter risks, and to survive more risk failures—whether they want to or not.

If you doubt this, please answer four questions:

1.   What changes do you worry about most when it comes to your job, career, and management work?

2.   What will you probably have to do that you fear doing to survive them?

3.   What dangers do these threatening changes create if you risk doing nothing about them?

4.   What opportunities do these threatening changes create if you risk doing something about them now?

Your answers may confirm the advisability of reconsidering your management practices so that you will more surely survive any disruptive change.

Risking takes on new meaning in confusing and chaotic times. No manager can afford to ignore the internal and external disarray that eventually threatens all work organizations. Nor can you or any other manager afford to dismiss the potential, if unsure, rewards of risk taking. Even if you hold a more sanguine outlook about the prevailing business climate, in the opinion of Jim Collins, coauthor of *Beyond Entrepreneurship* and lecturer at Stanford Business School, "Businesses need to take risks continually to survive over the long haul" (Collins, 1992).

WEATHERING RECESSIONARY CYCLES

Traditionally, risk avoidance promised the biggest, surest rewards for managers in both tough and easy times. Most organizations continue to reward management risk aversion, even when its practice leads to disastrous outcomes. During periods of economic difficulty, management's rallying cry becomes "Now is not the time to take any chances." During easier times, the litany remains unchanged: "Now that everything is going great why rock the boat with a risk we don't really have to take?"

Consider two cases in which managers won payoffs from risking in economically difficult times. The companies were Chrysler and Scandinavian Airlines. During one of Chrysler's worst business times ever, its management decided to develop the mini-van. By not playing it safe—that is, by not sticking to low-risk or no-risk product strategy—Chrysler reaped the rewards of creating a new market for a new product. The profits from this decision helped keep the firm alive financially during its ongoing battle to survive.

In the case of Scandinavian Airlines, chief executive Jan Carlzon used a counterintuitive, risk-taking strategy instead of a conventional, risk-avoidance one. While every European airline was gushing red ink, he rejected the course of cutting costs and services to restore profits: "I went to my board and presented a multi-million dollar plan to improve service quality, on the theory that the perceived difference between our competitors' declining service quality and our increasing service quality would steal market share. It worked." (Albrecht, 1992, p. 28).

While much of the time, including in crises, managers need to avoid taking chances, the missed opportunities for most managers are those risks they might actively seek, regardless of the circumstances or the dictates of conventional management thinking. Instead, most managers limit their risks to those that are compulsory and for which they usually won't be penalized. This excessively restrained strategy forfeits the vast rewards that could come from risking by choice, even when times are tough.

Those unwilling or unable to increase their risk-taking ante reduce the odds of surviving in economically sluggish periods. Will Rogers described it this way: "Even if you're on the right track, you'll get run over if you just sit there." Rogers's comically true warning applies equally to survival in career and business. Just staying employed as a manager or solvent as an organization seems an exceptional accomplishment.

Shying away from uncertainty can be a costly strategy for any organization. Take the case of Florida's Southeast Banking Corporation, a nonpareil financial institution with blue-chip customers. Southeast survived the Depression but ultimately lost out by avoiding changes it considered too risky, such as the consumer-banking boom. While it may survive, its story illustrates a rule that can be applied not only to the bankruptcy-plagued banking sector: "A basically stodgy institution can get into just as much trouble as a high flying one. And trying to do business as usual can be almost as risky as jumping on the latest industry bandwagon" (Brannigan, 1991, p. A-1).

UNLEASHING LEADERSHIP EXCELLENCE

The responsibilities of exceptional leadership, which include communicating an inspiring vision and challenging people to exceed status quo limits, all require discretionary risk taking. *Fortune* magazine identified the willingness and ability to take risks as one of seven leadership qualities distinguishing highly effective and respected senior managers and CEOs in the U.S. (Labich, 1988b). Those managers determined to be outstanding leaders will need to take more and larger risks than those whose aspirations are less ambitious. Leading others to produce outstanding results demands more voluntary risk taking than managers may yet realize.

Getting and keeping a larger share of the market or the profits is rare for managers who practice conservative leadership. This means pushing beyond customary limits of safety and comfort. Exceptional leaders gain greater rewards than risk-shy managers in part by taking risks more assertively and regularly.

Organizational survival and success hinge on management's skill and good fortune in making strategic decisions that involve potential gains and losses on a large scale: they include mergers, plant or office expansions, and closings, and are affected by major marketing shifts, changes in core business operations, and long-term planning and budgeting. These are risks "that cause returns to vary, that involve venturing into the unknown, and that may result in corporate ruin—all moves for which the outcomes and probabilities may be only partially known and where hard-to-define goals may not be met" (Baird and Thomas, 1985).

The necessity to excel at strategic-level risks may be particularly critical nowadays. That is the opinion of Peter Keen, for example, an international information technology consultant and author of several Harvard Business School books: "The necessity to take more and larger strategic-level risks has probably never been greater than today. Two worldwide business trends compel redefining strategic-level risk taking rules: first, pricing pressures are forcing down profit margins to lower levels, such as in the computer industry, creating additional strategic risks for businesses, no matter what they do; second, technology and productivity advances have led to worldwide overcapacity, generating yet more strategic risks in a flooded marketplace, both domestically and internationally" (Keen, 1991).

Successful management leaders carefully balance the costs of risking strategically by choice with those of risking reactively. Given the drawn-out time frame for strategic risks—usually several years—managers taking such actions voluntarily may gain critical time advantages. In contrast, managers refusing to do so at their own discretion may be compelled to play catch-up with new competitors, new technology, or new market forces.

A growing leadership test for managers is supporting subordinates' risk-taking ventures. As technology management consultant Lowell Christy reminds managers, the leadership role imposes special challenges on managers. In his view, management risk taking and "managing risk" differ significantly: "It takes one set of skills to take risks alone, by yourself, and another set of skills to lead a risk taking group, which is what 'managing risk' is about most of the time. Motivating yourself to risk, for example, is a whole different game from motivating your staff to take risks. Unless you know how to take risks, you're not going to do very well in managing risks" (1992). The good news is the potential double-win from leadership: winning once from enhancing your own risk-taking skills and winning a second time from doing the same for others.

GENERATING
EXCEPTIONAL PROFITS

An ironclad link connects a capitalistic economic system, profits, and management risk taking. Classical economists, for example, Adam Smith and John Stuart Mill, linked the rate of profit to the scale of risk taking. Even current management authorities, such as Peter Drucker, tie greater economic growth and progress to the willingness and ability to take greater risks.

Given that risks are the engines of economic growth in a capitalist economy, profits normally flow in direct proportion to the degree of risk. Smaller management risks typically generate smaller profits, fueling slower rates of growth. Larger management risks produce bigger profits, fueling faster growth. Depending on a firm's growth strategy, the necessity of making any kind of profit fuels and sustains management risk taking.

Generating high profits, not just marginal ones, supplies managers with a powerful reason to take optional risks. The faster you increase profits, the sooner you will pay off debt obligations. At the same time, your flexibility to invest in other profit-making ventures will increase. Lastly, your overall cash position will be stronger, allowing you to take advantage of new opportunities and meet unexpected costs. The profit rewards of risk taking result from applying two time-tested principles: (1) taking some risks precedes producing any profits, and (2) taking larger risks precedes producing larger profits.

The most profitable kinds of risks are called *dynamic risks* (Kehrer, 1989). In contrast to *static risks*, which leave things pretty much the way they were and preserve the status quo, dynamic risks abandon the past. They forge new ways of developing, making, and marketing products and services. They force large-scale change, forge new industries, launch new companies, and open new markets. They expand economic growth and create new jobs and careers. They "constantly revise and improve existing ways of doing things through the ultimate dynamic process we know as trial and error" (p. 3). When these risks fail, they fail on a large scale, just as when they succeed, they generate great progress and huge profits. These "vigorous and willfully under-taken risks are, in the words of one risk expert, the 'picks and shovels of enterprise'" (p. 4).

Dynamic risks are the breakthrough strategies that achieve high-gain management goals. Of necessity, they run counter to mainstream management thinking. They challenge the status quo, no matter how well it seems to be working or how uncertain the proposed improve-ments. The strategy may seem obvious or certain to have worked afterward, but beforehand, no one sees the pos-sibilities—no one, that is, except the courageous taker of dynamic management risks.

Until he died at age sixty-five in 1993, Steven J. Ross, mastermind in the creation of Time Warner, be-lieved risk taking was inherent in any business enter-prise. "If you're not a risk-taker," he is quoted as saying, "you should get the hell out of business" (Cohen, 1993, p. 1). Ross took huge risks on business opportunities, recognizing the worldwide potential of cable television, records, and videos long before his competitors. When other corporate leaders thought cable was just a rope of thick wire, he invested heavily in MTV and the Nickel-odeon cable service for children's programming.

DEVELOPING INNOVATIVE PRODUCTS AND SERVICES

Eventually, if not regularly, the growth and survival of every organization requires improved products and ser-

vices. Such improvements, whether subtle or radical, demand taking huge management risks related to talent,
time, budgets, technology, and other dwindling resources. "Risk is the backbone of new product development. It is the central core, the spinal cord, the brain
stem" (Kuczmarski, 1988, p. 15). For those willing to endure the risks come the largest payoffs from innovative
products and services.

Management risk takers understand how product
and service innovation represents one more area in
which new management realities call for new management rules. When they scan today's environment, they
grasp fully the management significance of changes
within it—changes that include cutthroat competition;
fickle, demanding customers and clients; narrower,
smaller, and faster-evolving market niches; and global
pressures for continuous quality improvement, to name
a few. All of them require taking greater-than-ever product and service risks.

Trying unconventional new methods of product development is one area in which certain kinds of payoffs
come only from voluntary risk taking. Compare, for example, IBM's traditional, slow, and standard new-
product strategy to Apple's quick and unorthodox approach to developing and launching new computer products. Neither company is in the financial clear at present,
but most would view Apple's riskier product development methods as more suited to the competitive environment in the computer industry.

Or consider Toshiba's overtly risky strategy of
flooding the market every few months with only slightly
different models of its computers. They keep those features that attract buyers and dump those that do not.
Unconventionality has worked as one of the new rules
in technology firms. This may be because the products
being manufactured are also unconventional: technologies and products thought impossible a few years before

are flourishing now, breaking old rules of risk taking (Feldman, 1986).

Risk takers advance innovation by indulging and tolerating the mistakes. With innovation, as with learning in general, a long string of failures precedes each eventual success. Both use new, unproven methods repeatedly until effective methods are found. If you accept more failure, however, you unlock and speed up innovation by getting the failures out of the way more quickly. But that means overcoming the stigma of management failure.

The logic of "failing forward," or dramatically speeding up the rate of failure to promote innovation, leads inevitably to increased risk taking and suggests the following rules: (1) every organization needs to innovate faster in every area; (2) innovation deals with new and untested ideas and methods discovered only through failure; (3) to innovate faster yields more frequent innovation failures; (4) speeded-up risk taking dramatically increases the number of failures yielding speeded-up innovation (Peters, 1987b, p. 260). The caveat, of course, is that you learn from the failures, a tactic discussed in Chapter Eight.

There is some reason to believe not only that risk taking supports quality improvement but also that the reverse is true: a quality-driven work culture encourages employees to take risks more often and managers to reward that behavior more generously. The Ritz Carlton Hotel chain, one of the 1992 winners of the Malcolm Baldrige Award for Quality, may have uncovered the tie between implementing quality improvements and stimulating employee attitudes toward their risk taking (Ritz Carlton, 1991). The percentage of employees expressing positive attitudes about the extent to which management rewarded their risk taking increased substantially as the hotels implemented far-reaching quality improvements. Ritz Carlton data suggest that at least one of the payoffs of continuous improvements in quality may be continuous improvements in employee satisfaction with the rewards of risk taking.

MANAGING TECHNOLOGY COMPETITIVELY

There are abundant if unguaranteed rewards for risking to manage technology more competitively. These kinds of risks might include reworking procedures for developing and distributing new products; investing in newer facilities and equipment and in worker training; and forming new alliances with competitors.

In technology-dependent organizations, which all organizations are to some degree, managing technology effectively pays unquestioned dividends; that is, if managers are willing to assume the dangers involved. Those amenable to doing so have a shot at gaining an edge that translates into profits. Consider this manufacturing example: "The willingness of [Pacific Rim manufacturers], particularly in Japan, to take well-calculated risks has put American factory managers in double jeopardy. First, Pacific Rim factories are gaining new technologies from their risk taking ventures, and second, they are progressing around the learning curve faster than we because they have raised their level of expectations through risk taking" (Shamlin, 1989, p. 65).

Service organizations, too, can realize bottom-line benefits from discretionary technology risks, such as the early purchase of new telecommunications technology. (While the leading edge can certainly deteriorate into the bleeding edge—or bleeding red ink—so can inefficient or outdated equipment and methods.) On a more personal level, managers who introduce new technology, or an innovative application of it, often create promising new career paths for themselves—or at least enhance their marketability in a difficult job market.

An increasingly technology-intensive workplace requires rewriting the rules of management risk taking. MCI, for example, is constantly taking technology risks. MCI senior vice president Carol Herod (1992) describes some of the ones she confronts in her own position: "My work involves managing a lot of technology risks: risks of estimating incorrectly the amount of time it takes to develop and deliver the technology supporting a new service; risks of our vendors not delivering what they promised or delivering it on time; and risks that our pre-release testing will uncover major design or operating errors, causing us to have to go back to the design boards."

Sweeping changes are mandating broad revisions in risk-taking guidelines. They include shrinking time frames for technology development, escalating capital-investment costs of research, and the dwindling life spans of the scientific foundations of technology.

The potential benefits of rethinking the ground rules for technology innovation risks are immense, since those innovations have accounted for about one-half our economic growth. The uncertain but extensive advantages of risking for technological payoffs belong, more often than not, to those who walk the highwire of risk.

ACHIEVING EXTRAORDINARY CAREER GOALS

Career advancement nearly always involves some measure of risk. Whatever your current career goal, be it a higher position, a higher salary, or simply more meaningful work, taking an intentional risk to achieve it can deliver satisfying payoffs. They include not only open, public ones, such as greater respect and recognition, but also private, personal ones like pride and confidence. Even managers who fail in these risks still value their courage and convictions over any resulting penalties.

Research supports the good sense and practicality of taking management risks in pursuit of higher career goals. Those who have become CEOs, for example, have histories of risk taking. They expect a share of career victories and defeats. But they also recognize the need to continue taking risks while seeking toeholds in the climb to the next level. Managers unwilling to do so are unlikely to turn their career dreams into reality except by luck or accident.

IMPLEMENTING QUALITY IMPROVEMENTS SUCCESSFULLY

Some managers question the value of what is called *total quality management* (TQM), *continuous quality improvement,* or *total quality.* In brief, TQM is a set of quality-driven management values, principles, and methods. In practice, TQM focuses on such strategies as meeting and exceeding customer expectations, preventing problems from happening routinely, basing decisions on recent data, involving employees and suppliers in improving productivity and service by improving the processes that produce them, and similar quality-creating practices.

TQM has attracted many defenders and believers, along with many critics and skeptics. Whatever one's attitude toward TQM, it seems fairly certain that TQM, or something close to it, must occur soon if America is to remain a dominant force in the world economy of the coming decades. What is becoming increasingly clear in the rearview mirror of experience implementing TQM, however, is how risk-filled TQM is when the rubber of implementation hits the road of quality.

TQM offers its envied if seldom achieved rewards when managers take risks—voluntary risks like embarking on a never-ending and grueling quest for new frontiers of quality; voluntary risks like changing leadership practices, perhaps by choosing to coach instead of command others.

When managers and their organizations get beyond the hype of much TQM planning and the fluff of much TQM training, when they get down to actually using the principles and methods of TQM, many of them want to call it quits. And it's understandable, given the large and frequent risks TQM involves—risks like investing tens of thousands of dollars in training programs and seeing quality stay the same; risks like committing to TQM only to have top managers who vowed they were "100 percent supportive," refuse to come through with time, money, or changes in their own quality-limiting behavior; risks like bringing a quality improvement opportunity to the attention of higher management and being rebuked for it; and risks like giving up some of your most cherished management principles in order to meet the demands of TQM.

There are some common problems in organization-wide implementation of TQM and the practice of responsible management risk taking. Both require the complete commitment and constant involvement of top management; both involve the uncovering of opportunities by taking planned actions and learning from the outcomes; and both go against the grain of current management principles and practices.

Both TQM and risk taking are long-term strategies. Risk taking as a management strategy works most effectively, just as TQM does, when used correctly and consistently over the years. Many risks (and many quality improvements) will prove justified only in the long haul.

Fear of risk taking prevents many if not most organizations from enjoying the numerous benefits of successfully implemented TQM. Leading experts on quality agree about the high cost of fear in the workplace. In *Driving Fear Out of the Workplace,* authors Kathleen Ryan and Daniel Oestreich (1991) explain how fear saps any extra effort, causes people to hide mistakes, reverses priorities, and leads to a decrease in risk taking. Their research documents how the failure to reward those taking TQM risks—challenging sacred procedures, for example, or volunteering to lead a quality team—denies organizations their own TQM rewards of increased efficiencies or customer retention.

Some quality experts estimate that as few as 5 to 10 percent of American businesses will risk developing and sustaining the discipline, commitment, and involvement that TQM demands from every employee, and especially managers. Only those willing to risk actively, intentionally, and regularly will ever enjoy the countless and well-documented payoffs of TQM. Such payoffs include increasing profits by as much as 5 to 10 percent of sales in the manufacturing sector and 30 percent in the service sector; the elimination of waste and rework; higher customer retention rates and greater pride in one's work. The list could go on.

MANAGING WITH GUSTO

The most common and personal reward for risking by preference may be the satisfaction of complying with your internal value system—risking because it reflects your convictions about what ultimately matters most to you as a manager. These often stubborn but always principled motivations yield psychological or moral payoffs, such as experiencing an inner pride and heightened self-esteem for acting according to your own credo.

Those who value adventurous and heart-felt risk taking, if only for its intangible rewards, display a rare gusto for it. Literally speaking, *gusto* is a four-hundred-year-old word meaning "hearty or keen enjoyment" (*Random House Dictionary*). Gusto has far deeper significance for management risk taking than television commercials once claimed it had for beer. In a more sober context, "going for the gusto" means bringing maximum enjoyment and self-fulfillment to your management career without compromising your values. Gusto risk takers agree with Booz-Allen & Hamilton vice president Joyce Doria that one of the best possible reasons to take risks as a manager is to find out just how good you really are (1992).

In his novel *Zorba the Greek*, Nikos Kazantzakis (1952) writes about a larger-than-life character who responds with zeal and zest to all life offers him, whether painful or pleasurable. Zorba-like managers risk for the gusto of it, at least in part.

In quieter, less dramatic, and less publicized ways, management Zorbas assert and defend their right to risk according to their convictions and commitments. Real-world examples of male Zorbas might include people like Bill Gates (Microsoft), Steve Jobs (Apple Computer), Jack Welch (General Electric), and Bill McGowin (MCI). Female examples are people like Carol Bartz (Auto Desk, Inc.), Kathleen Black (*USA Today*), Ellen Marram (Nabisco Biscuit Company) or Marian Wright Edelman (Children's Defense Fund). These and other gusto-impelled managers choose action over cynicism, commitment over pessimism, "I tried . . ." over "If only . . ." They believe in the net advantages of not just ordinary risk taking but a passionate, principled, persistent, fire-in-the-belly version of it.

How they handle defeat distinguishes Zorba-style

risk takers from others. Notice how Zorba deals with the devastating failure of a grand, against-the-odds, all-or-nothing business venture:

> This time I had lost everything—my money, my men, the line, the trucks; we had constructed a small port and now we had nothing to export. It was all lost.
>
> Well, it was precisely at that moment that I felt an unexpected sense of deliverance. As if in the hard, somber labyrinth of necessity I had discovered liberty herself playing happily in a corner. And I played with her.
>
> When everything goes wrong, what a joy to test your soul and see if it has endurance and courage! An invisible and all-powerful enemy . . . seems to rush upon us to destroy us; but we are not destroyed.
>
> Each time . . . we are the conquerors, although externally utterly defeated, we human beings feel an indescribable pride and joy. Outward calamity is transformed into a supreme and unshakable felicity [Kazantzakis, 1952, pp. 291–292].

Just like Zorba, those who manage with gusto refuse to let defeat lessen the intense pleasures and inconstant rewards of their risks. They bear their scars, both visible and unseen, with pride and dignity and without apologizing or bragging.

Managing with gusto means, for instance, feeling pleased and contented at your retirement party. It is refusing to end your professional life feeling unfulfilled, empty, or regretful, as does George Gray, speaking from his grave in the poem by Edgar Lee Masters:

> I have studied many times
> The marble which was chiseled for me—
> A boat with a furled sail at rest in a harbor.

In truth it pictures not my destination
But my life . . .
Ambition called to me, but I dreaded the chances.
Yet all the while I hungered for meaning in my life.
And now I know that we must lift the sail
And catch the winds of destiny
Wherever they drive the boat.
To put meaning in one's life may end in madness,
But life without meaning is the torture
Of restlessness and vague desire—
It is a boat longing for the sea and yet afraid.
(Edgar Lee Masters, *The Spoon River Anthology*)

Gusto-motivated managers shun the hesitation and meekness of a George Gray. They embrace the boldness and defiance of Zorba. Even when bruised or broken by their risks, management Zorbas live out their careers in purposeful and vigorous pursuit of risk-blocked goals. They travel the path of greatest resistance because they know it usually leads to the greatest rewards. Regardless of how their risks turn out, at least they never have to experience wistful regrets.

PART TWO

Building Strong
Risk-Taking Skills

3

ASSESS YOUR BOUNDARIES, TRAITS, AND ASSUMPTIONS

Risk-taking mastery begins with self-assessment—appraising your risk-taking beliefs and perceptions. This first step toward risk mastery requires only about a half hour or so to read this chapter and complete three self-inventories. Be prepared to appraise yourself honestly.

DISCOVER YOUR RISK-TAKING QUALITIES

A truthful self-assessment improves your risk mastery in several ways. First, it assesses your risk-taking traits. What qualities and attitudes displayed by effective risk takers do you have already, and which ones do you need to develop? Second, it measures how your need to be in control of your risks influences your willingness to take financial risks. Third, it affirms or contests your assumptions about the long-term consequences of risk taking for managers' careers. If, for instance, you believe it is rare for a manager who initiates risks to get to the top and you possess that ambition, you are less likely to be open to taking optional management risks yourself. And fourth, it reveals several widespread myths about risk taking. These myths bias your risk decisions and actions, endangering you and your organization. In sum, these self-assessment tools help you strengthen and develop the beliefs, attitudes, and skills of risk-taking mastery.

When you do the exercises in this chapter, view the results as feedback, rather than as a scientific diagnosis of your risk taking. Forego labeling yourself permanently as a risk taker or risk avoider. Instead, use the exercises to credit yourself with your risk-taking assets and to motivate yourself to correct your risk-taking deficits. Resist second-guessing the "right" answers, as this distorts the feedback and weakens its value in identifying areas of growth with the greatest payoffs for you. Use these tools as a starting point for building your risk-taking skills. Allow them to become a springboard for your growth as a risk taker.

INVENTORY YOUR
RISK-TAKING ATTITUDES

While no particular set of attitudes consistently distinguishes all risk takers from avoiders, research data and expert opinion suggest many of the ways in which they frequently differ. Exercise 3.1 will help you determine which risk-taking attitudes you possess. Completing the exercise will increase your awareness of attitudes you do and do not share with active risk takers.

The higher your score, the more your risk-taking attitudes resemble those of risk takers studied by social scientists. A score of about 11 or higher indicates strong to very strong pro-risk attitudes; about 6 to 10, medium strength pro-risk attitudes; and 5 or less, low strength pro-risk attitudes.

Exercise 3.1. Risk Attitudes Inventory.

Read each trait description. Assess yourself on the basis of the degree to which the trait description applies to you (most of the time) in your management work and circle the appropriate answer. Be aware that looking for hidden meanings will not improve the value of your self-rating. Your first reaction is probably your best. A guide for scoring and interpreting your responses follows the exercise.

1. Taking management risks makes good sense only in the absence of acceptable alternatives. Agree Disagree

2. I generally prefer stimulation over security. Agree Disagree

3. I have confidence in my ability to recover from my mistakes, no matter how big. Agree Disagree

4. I would promote someone with unlimited potential but limited experience to a key position over someone with limited potential but more experience. Agree Disagree

5. Anything worth doing is worth doing less than perfectly. Agree Disagree

6. I believe opportunity generally knocks only once. Agree Disagree

7. It is better to ask for permission than to beg for forgiveness. Agree Disagree

8. Success in management is as much a matter of luck as ability. Agree Disagree

9. Given a choice, I would choose a three-thousand-dollar annual raise over a ten-thousand-dollar bonus, which I had about a one-in-three chance of winning. Agree Disagree

10. I can handle big losses and disappointments with little difficulty. Agree Disagree

11. If forced to choose between them, I would take safety over achievement. Agree Disagree

12. Failure is the long way to management success. Agree Disagree

13. I tolerate ambiguity and unpredictability well. Agree Disagree

14. I would rather feel intense disappointment than intense regret. Agree Disagree

Exercise 3.1. Risk Attitudes Inventory, Cont'd.

15. When facing a decision with uncertain conse-
     quences, my potential losses are my greatest
     concern.   Agree Disagree

*Give yourself one point for each of the following statements with
which you agree: 2, 3, 4, 5, 10, 13, 14. Give yourself one point for
each of the following statements with which you disagree: 1, 6, 7, 8,
9, 11, 12, 15. Calculate your total.*

Source: Highwire Management by Gene Calvert. Copyright
© 1993 by Jossey-Bass Publishers. Permission to reproduce and distribute material (with copyright notice visible) is hereby granted. If
material is to be used in a compilation to be sold for profit, please
contact the publisher for permission.

Your score will tell you more about your risk-taking
attitudes when you compare your responses with those
of a risk taker. Someone giving a pro-risk response on all
inventory items would agree with the following beliefs
and assumptions about risk taking, which correspond to
the items in the inventory:

1. Risk by choice, not just by necessity; chosen risks
    usually benefit you much more than forced ones.

2. Security is a myth; professional stimulation (chal-
    lenge, growth, or excitement) is worth the cost.

3. A way out of almost any risk-taking problem can
    probably be found or created, including a way to
    survive "the worst," if it actually happens.

4. Conventional personnel management practices like
    promoting someone on the basis of past experience,
    produce average results, if more certain perfor-
    mance; unconventional management practices like
    promoting someone on the basis of his or her poten-
    tial, produce unconventional results, such as out-
    standing, if less certain, performance.

5. Risk taking is typically a messy, fast-moving, make-it-up-as-you-go, very imperfect process, no matter how well you plan or implement it; waiting until you can risk near-perfectly means seldom risking, or missing the best window of opportunity for risking.

6. No matter how many times your risks fail, there will always be another opportunity to risk again, and perhaps succeed the next time. The ratio of wins to losses matters little in the end. Risk takers know that what counts most is the net value of wins as compared to losses in an acceptable period of time, such as a budget cycle or an average time span at a management position or level.

7. While getting permission is always a smart approach, some management risks have to be launched without prior approval; if it succeeds, no apologies are needed; it the risk fails, and it was legitimate and responsibly undertaken, you will probably be forgiven anyway.

8. Luck always helps, but you create your own luck by taking risks and betting on yourself. Your own ability contributes to making things happen the way you want them to happen. As the state lottery ad puts it, "You have to play to win"; for managers, that means taking risks and not depending on random circumstances, events, or other people.

9. The bigger the risk, the bigger the reward, so go for the riskier choice if it offers a greater payoff; believe in your own ability to produce results, especially when you have pivotal control of the outcome, as with your job performance.

10. Failure and loss should be viewed as learning experiences that will pay off in the long term. What you learn from your risk-taking mistakes is what makes

risks worth taking. Learning anything new is a matter of doing things wrong until you get them right.

11. For a manager or an organization, achieving anything worthwhile requires venturing into unsafe territory. Being satisfied with average achievements, a standard of mediocrity, allows you to stick with the safe, sure, and secure; being dissatisfied with anything less than outstanding, a standard of excellence, forces you to relinquish the safe, sure, and secure.

12. Succeeding as a manager means having a modest share of failures, if only because producing outstanding results requires taking risks, many of which will fail. The trick is not to fail too catastrophically.

13. Ambiguity and unpredictability permeate and complicate risk taking; those able to cope with these constraints will do well at risk taking, or at least better than those who can't.

14. You always feel good about yourself when you risk sensibly and boldly, even when you fail, for you sustain and expand your self-esteem and earn the respect of others. Risking and then failing means never having to blame yourself for lacking the courage to try. Better to feel the disappointments of risking than the regrets of not risking.

15. When risking, keep one eye on the potential losses and one on the potential gains, instead of focusing obsessively on what you can lose. Risk to secure gains, as well as to prevent losses.

VERIFY YOUR
RISK CONTROL NEEDS

Exercise 3.2 measures needing to feel in control when taking risks (Rotter, 1971, p. 42). This force-choice scale assumes that a greater sense of internal control facili-

Exercise 3.2. Risk-Taking Control Scale.

For each item, choose one of the two alternatives. The scoring key is below the questions.

I strongly believe that:

____ Promotions are earned through hard work and persistence.

____ In my experience I have noticed that there was usually a direct connection between how hard I studied and the grades I got.

____ The number of divorces indicates that more and more people are not trying to make their marriages work.

____ When I am right I can convince others.

____ In our society a man's future earning power is dependent upon his ability.

____ If one knows how to deal with people they are really quite easily led.

____ In my case the grades I made were the results of my own efforts; luck had little or nothing to do with it.

____ People like me can change the course of world affairs if we make ourselves heard.

____ I am the master of my fate.

____ Getting along with people is a skill that must be practiced.

I believe strongly that:

____ Making a lot of money is largely a matter of getting the right breaks.

____ Many times the reactions of teachers seemed haphazard to me.

____ Marriage is largely a gamble.

____ It is silly to think that one can really change another person's basic attitudes.

____ Getting promoted is really a matter of being a little luckier than the next guy.

____ I have little influence over the way other people behave.

____ Sometimes I feel that I had little to do with the grades I got.

____ It is only wishful thinking to believe that one can really influence what happens in society at large.

____ A great deal that happens to me is probably a matter of chance.

____ It is almost impossible to figure out how to please some people.

Source: Adapted from Rotter, J. "External Control and Internal Control." *Psychology Today,* June 1971, p. 42. Reprinted by permission in *Highwire Management* by Gene Calvert. Copyright © 1993 by Jossey-Bass Publishers. Permission to reproduce and distribute material should be obtained from J. Rotter.

tates risk taking. Having more confidence in your own ability to control events may incline you to risk more in quest of rewards. Selecting more alternatives on the left suggests stronger internal control needs; selecting more from the right suggests stronger external control needs.

UPDATE YOUR RISK
SUCCESS ASSUMPTIONS

Exercise 3.3 summarizes the patterns and key practices of successful management risk takers. It allows you to compare your assumptions about them with the expertise of risk-taking authorities and data from recent risk research.

The quiz challenges assumptions you might have about whether risk taking pays off in the long run. Do managers who risk by choice and with some regularity end up better or worse off than managers who mostly avoid risks throughout their careers? How do risk-taking managers view the role of luck in their risks? Does your being male or female make a difference in your risk-taking patterns?

This exercise brings to light, for example, how some of your expectations about what happens to fellow management risk takers may limit your willingness and ability to join them. Your agreement or disagreement with specific quiz items, regardless of their reasoning or data, should not distract you from the overall value of the exercise: prompting you to reexamine and revise your risk-taking strategy in light of the collective experience of managers generally, based on current scientific evidence and expert opinion. Please answer the quiz now.

1. *Do managers who are more successful take more risks?* Studies conducted with different management groups at different times for over thirty years confirm greater risk taking among managers who are more suc-

Exercise 3.3. Risk Success Quiz.

Circle the answer you think is best for each statement. You will get the most out of this exercise if you answer the quiz first, score your answers, and then read the explanations. The answers appear at the end of the quiz.

1.	Managers who are more successful take more risks than managers who are less successful.	True	False
2.	Female managers risk differently than male managers.	True	False
3.	Managers driven to high achievement take high risks frequently.	True	False
4.	High fear of failure inhibits taking high management risks.	True	False
5.	Skill matters more than chance in taking large or small risks.	True	False
6.	Managers who are more experienced take fewer risks than managers who are less experienced.	True	False
7.	Managers with more authority take more risks than managers with less authority.	True	False
8.	Managers in larger firms take more risks than managers in smaller firms.	True	False
9.	Managers with graduate degrees, such as M.B.A.'s, take more risks than those who do not have graduate degrees.	True	False
10.	Most managers are risk averse.	True	False

Answers: 1. True; 2. True (maybe); 3. False; 4. False; 5. False; 6. True; 7. True; 8. False; 9. True; 10. True.

Source: Highwire Management by Gene Calvert. Copyright © 1993 by Jossey-Bass Publishers. Permission to reproduce and distribute material (with copyright notice visible) is hereby granted. If material is to be used in a compilation to be sold for profit, please contact the publisher for permission.

cessful. Chief executive officers and chief operating officers, for example, have taken more risks than those not reaching this management pinnacle. They see themselves as greater risk takers, as compared to other senior managers. A team of business school professors studied hundreds of senior managers and found that the most successful of them had taken more management risks than the others. Success was measured several ways: by managers' positions, firm size, directorships held, and personal wealth (MacCrimmon and Wehrung, 1986). The positive, and perhaps critical, impact of risk-taking practices on managers' success holds true regardless of which measure of success was used.

Managers who rise to the top have made it, in part, because they take more risks. Not all of their risks work out well. Yet they certainly had to take some en route to higher positions, larger salaries, and bigger firms. Their risk-taking practices also helped move them up the organizational ladder more rapidly than their peers. Some psychologists believe that a willingness to take risks is an early sign of future success, according to Kehrer (1989). A Hay and Associates study of the promotion histories and risk-taking practices of over seven hundred managers in one large multinational company supports this conclusion (Grey and Gordon, 1978).

The trick, if there is one, may be to take calculated, modest- to medium-sized risks, and a moderate number of them. Taking balanced risks is characteristic of managers with successful careers. They are not super-cautious, so they are able to stand out and move up. Nor are they so super-reckless that they fall off the promotional ladder.

Several factors account for greater risk-taking differences among more successful managers as compared with other managers: they take more risks in general, if more selectively; most of their risks have worked out well, for whatever reasons; they favor moderate-scale risks, but take large-scale risks when they feel they must; and they take more risks earlier in their careers than do managers who take fewer risks. Managers who are more successful may or may not possess greater management competence. But they have taken and survived more risks.

Managers who are less successful may have made a different risk trade-off, choosing career security over career advancement. As a result, they may have moved up the career ladder more slowly, stayed in dead-end positions longer, and ended up at lower management levels than more risk-active managers.

With equal possibility, less successful managers may have taken too many risks, or ones that were too dangerous, blocking or limiting their advancement early in their careers. Their carelessness or bad luck may have permanently limited their career prospects, prompting them to switch to other career fields.

In risk taking, as in so many other endeavors, moderation pays the most reliable dividends. Extremely careless risk takers get moved out of their organization or field, whether voluntarily or involuntarily. Extremely cautious risk takers fare little better, given the small number of risk-averse managers who reach higher management circles. (This does not contradict the strong risk aversion often seen among managers once they reach top-level positions.) As a general pattern, managers risking excessively err toward losing out, and those who are totally averse to risking tend to plateau out.

2. *Do female managers risk differently than male managers?* The answer, based on current research, is yes . . . and no. Research indicates that both women and men believe women risk less often. Yet in actual practice, female managers risk just as frequently as do male managers (MacCrimmon and Wehrung, 1986).

Women and men tend to find different explanations for their risk-taking successes and failures. Women, for instance, tend to attribute their failures to themselves, focusing, for example, on lack of ability or insufficient effort. Men are just the opposite. They tend to attribute their failures to external events, such as lack of time and insufficient help. In general, according to one summary of research on these differences, "men internalize and accept responsibility for successes, and women internalize and accept responsibility for failure" (Marone, 1992, p. 66).

Long-term research confirms that there are many more similarities than differences in the risk-taking behavior of men and women, both inside and outside in the workplace (Siegelman, 1983; Jensen, 1981). Results of this research also contradict the commonly held view of female managers—and women in general—as more conservative risk takers. In studying the investment preferences of men and women, for example, investment security needs were the same for men and women (Blum, 1976). But the conclusions of present research are open to debate (as research always is, of course); they may not yet reflect the most complete and up-to date information about female risk taking in the workplace. A number of unresearched gender-related differences may exist, such as a greater willingness of female managers to take risks that are interpersonal, rather than career-based, at work (Siegleman, 1983; Kehrer, 1989). These women may also give more weight to the personal and family ramifications of workplace risks, like job transfers and promotions (Kehrer, 1989).

A number of issues distort our current understanding of the differences between male and female risk taking, as well as our knowledge of their causes and significance . Such factors as gender discrimination and organizational culture may deny women access to positions that have the authority and command the resources required for the level of risk taking they seek. Recent data on small-business start-ups show more female than male entrepreneurs, suggesting that women may be more willing, or may find it more necessary, taking strategies to achieve career goals denied them in the corporate world.

Some women managers see their own risk taking as different from that of men. Several differences are noted by Rebecca Klemm, president and founder of a research and policy analysis firm:

Generally speaking, I think women managers differ in some ways from male managers as risk takers. The same management risks, for example, are often more emotional for women than for men. From many conversations with other women executives, I do know we don't walk away emotionally from our risk experiences nearly as quickly or as easily as men seem to.

My perception is women agonize more about the human aftermath of management risks, like how they affect the personal lives of the people they manage. I'm not saying men don't. It may be that women just worry more verbally, openly, or frankly about human fallout issues than male managers, generally.

I also think women managers fret and stew more about how their risks will be seen by other managers, their bosses or customers especially. I believe women take more risks because they have to—we have to do more, invest more, attempt more, and prove more to get the same rewards as men. "You've come a long way, baby" means women have taken one heck of a lot of risk taking in the business world [Klemm, 1992].

Dona Wolf, director of the U.S. Office of Personnel Management's Human Resources Development Group, notes changes in the risk environment for women: "Today's environment is much more conducive to risk taking for women managers, thanks in part to equal opportunity laws and other changing cultural values. I believe, for instance, women risk takers are more visible today. That's both good and bad news for women managers. If your risk succeeds, your success is more noticeable, but if your risk fails, it too is more conspicuous. I think women have both more to gain, and more to lose, from taking management risks" (Wolf, 1992).

3. *Does the need for high achievement lead to taking higher risks?* Managers who are oriented toward

high achievement tend to take medium-level risks. They avoid what they define as high-level risks that are beyond their grasp. At the same time, they avoid low-level risks that provide little sense of accomplishment. As achievement-driven managers generally like to be in control, they typically avoid risks in which chance seems likely to determine the outcome (Bem, 1980).

4. *Does fear of failure inhibit risk taking?* Managers with a high fear of failure are less likely to take moderate-risks. Instead, they tend to take either high risks or very low ones for different reasons: big risks impose a limited sense of responsibility, since no one has complete control over their outcome; little risks cause little anxiety, since their potential losses are small. The potent and underestimated effects of fear on management risk taking are detailed in Chapter Six.

5. *Does skill matter more than chance in risk taking?* Every risk involves elements of both skill and chance. How much of the risk-taking outcome depends on skill and how much on chance is far more a matter of belief than of evidence. You have no way of knowing with certainty before the fact which factor will prove most critical in the end.

Despite this, your before-the-fact beliefs about the power of skill versus that of chance have an influence on your risk decision. Research shows that belief in the power of skill to determine the outcome increases the willingness to take moderate risks. It does not, however, increase the willingness to take large or small risks.

In contrast, believing that chance determines the risk outcome has the effect of decreasing the tendency to take moderate risks. In addition, believing strongly in chance factors increases the tendency to take very large or very small risks. A number of risk-taking tactics mitigate the always pivotal role of chance in risking, as discussed in Chapters Seven and Eight.

In sum, when skill seems paramount, managers are

more likely to take moderate risks. But when chance seems paramount, managers are more likely to take either expanded risks or much smaller risks (Kogan and Wallach, 1967; Bem, 1980).

6. *Do managers who are more experienced risk less often?* Managers who are more experienced take fewer risks than those who are less experienced (Vroom and Pahl, 1971). While current research fails to explain why, a number of factors may account for this greater risk-taking conservatism. Those who are more seasoned may, perhaps, know better the large number of variables operative in any risk venture. They may have more to lose and less to gain from risk taking. They may have less time in their careers to recover from tragic risk outcomes. Finally, they may have greater personal responsibilities, like elderly parents or children attending college.

7. *Do managers with more authority take more risks?* Managers with greater authority take more risks than those with less authority (MacCrimmon and Wehrung, 1986). CEOs and other chief operating officers typically risk more than senior managers, and senior managers in turn risk more than middle managers. In addition, the higher their authority, the more managers will be likely to see themselves as risk takers. Their self-image, therefore, matches their actual behavior. It may be, of course, that past success with risk taking has helped them reach higher levels of authority, which in turn supports further risk taking.

CEOs have taken and survived enough right risks to make it to the head of an organization. Those who take careless risks or who are extremely risk averse rarely become CEOs, or don't survive long if they do. Greater risk taking among CEOs has nothing to do with seniority or firm size. "Seniority" refers to how long you've been with the firm, not your position in it. Recent research, for instance, found that "the inclination to encourage others to take risks increased as one moved up the hierarchy" (March and Shapira, 1987, pp. 1404–1418).

Looking at the other end of the management hierarchy, mid-level managers, generally speaking, tend to be considerably more risk averse than more senior managers. This tendency may reflect their more limited decision-making discretion and span of control, or it may reflect other factors, like an extremely risk-averse boss or organization.

Organizations with bureaucratic cultures that stifle risk taking by middle managers hurt themselves strategically. As one study concluded, "most middle managers in bureaucratic organizations shun risks that, from the overall company point of view, would be very attractive" (Hunsaker, 1975, pp. 173–185).

8. *Do managers in larger firms take more risks?* Managers in larger firms tend to believe they risk just as frequently as managers in smaller firms. Research shows just the opposite to be the case. Managers in larger firms actually take fewer risks than managers in smaller firms (MacCrimmon and Wehrung, 1986). Qualities inherent in larger organizations, such as more decision-making layers or more conservative management methods, may put more constraints on risk taking than are found in smaller organizations. Managers in smaller organizations, however, report taking significantly more risks, perhaps due to greater opportunity, but perhaps out of necessity as well.

A high percentage of managers in small, entrepreneurial organizations, as compared to managers in larger, less entrepreneurial ones, view themselves as risk takers. Roughly one-half of those questioned in a survey said they "like the thrill of going for it all," and about one-fourth "like to take some chances" or opt for "only calculated risks." For those owning their businesses, the larger the business, the less likely it is that owners opt for "the thrill of going for it all" (Pollock and Pollock, 1986, p. 24).

9. *Do managers with graduate degrees risk more?* Managers with master's degrees in any subject tend to take more risks than those with bachelor's degrees or high school credentials. No measurable difference occurs in the risk-taking frequency of managers with or without bachelor's degrees. Managers with high school diplomas risk just as often as those with college degrees.

Just what factors account for greater risk taking among managers with graduate degrees is unknown. The largest and most recent study of management risk takers speculates that "higher education is not responsible for the spark that initiates risk taking. But it doesn't extinguish the flame, either" (MacCrimmon and Wehrung, 1986, pp. 249–250).

10. *Are most managers risk avoiders?* Regardless of your answer to the quiz, ask yourself what ballpark percentage of managers see themselves as risk takers: 50 percent? 10 percent? 30 percent? Both common sense and current research suggest that a large proportion of managers avoid all optional risks. My estimate is that about three-fourths do. This suggests that a minority of managers take voluntary risks on a regular basis or on a significant scale. Perhaps twice as many managers, about 50 percent or so, probably qualify as risk takers by their beliefs, but not by their behavior.

Three aspects of risk taking make it difficult to know just how many managers are primarily risk avoiders and how many are risk seekers: the situational, relative, and subjective nature of risk taking.

First, the situational nature of risk means you may or may not take a type of risk, such as ethically debatable marketing tactics, depending on the exact circumstances. Second, risks are relative in that you differ from other managers in your risk comfort zones; the risks you routinely take may be out of the question for other managers, and vice versa. And third, active risk takers rarely label themselves as such, in part because their risk decisions and actions do not seem terribly risky to them. In a very real sense then, all managers are risk takers in certain circumstances, with certain risks, and with certain levels of risk-taking awareness.

The percentage of managers who are risk takers may be about the same as the percentage of risk-takers in the general population. University of Wisconsin psychologist Frank Farley estimates that about 30 percent of Americans are true risk takers. These are the serious, regular, experimental, rule-breaking, entrepreneurial risk takers from all walks of life (Skrzycki and others, 1987).

JETTISON THE MYTHS

Mistaken beliefs and assumptions about risk taking can seriously harm you and your organization. What is worse, they can lock you into weaker, less effective risk tactics. You can minimize the likelihood of this by jettisoning four common myths about management risk taking.

Myth Number One: Not Risking Is Not Risking

This myth rests on the assumption that risk inaction assures greater safety most if not all of the time—that the potential dangers of risking will always surpass those of not risking. If you believe that avoiding risks protects you from preventable harm and that taking them exposes you to unpreventable harm, why take risks? Because risk inaction does have potential penalties: stunted or delayed professional growth, slowed or plateaued career progress, lost opportunities to innovate, lost market share if competitors succeed at risks you rejected, and regret at mid-life or retirement for the doors you never tried to open, and so on.

The conclusion: not risking is still risking. Not risking is simply taking a different kind of risk: the passive risk of inaction. A qualitative divide separates risks you take knowingly and intentionally (active risking) and risks you face unknowingly (passive risking). When you risk actively, you may permit or create the possibility that something unneeded or unwanted will happen—for example, the failure of a new product or service. When you risk passively, you prevent something needed or wanted from occurring—increased revenues, for example, from a new product or service.

Passive risks occur in two forms: not risking by conscious choice (with an awareness of the downside dangers of this decision); and unconsciously failing to decide or act (without an awareness of the downside dangers of this "decision"). Risk-taking inaction or passiveness is simply another, possibly more expensive, kind of risking.

You succumb to this myth, for instance, when you assume that avoiding a voluntary career change promises more security than changing careers. Yet consider how many hundreds of thousands of managers—middle managers in particular—have tumbled from career complacency to career catastrophe in the last decade by believing this myth. Even what seemed to be the most protected professions—medicine, law, and banking—no longer offer immunity to career malaise, burnout, and obsolescence.

Excessive reliance on passive risk taking means that too many resources will be used to prevent losses and too few to achieve gains. Consider, for instance, an organization that loses its market share in tough times simply by failing to expand aggressively in good times. Active risking tries to expand and improve an organization but may fail at great cost. Passive risking tries to keep the organization just where it is but may also fail at great cost.

Part of the error of believing "not risking is not risking" stems from betting that the status quo will remain the status quo—that your risk situation will stay pretty much the way it is now. Despite countless highly publicized warnings, from those in *Future Shock* over twenty years ago to the predictions in *Megatrends* more recently, some managers still cling to this belief. This is puzzling given the evidence of growing instability. The *Wall Street Journal, Fortune,* and *Forbes* are filled with gloomy tales of those living amid anarchic change who lost their playing-it-safe bet on the status quo.

In reality, the possibility of risk persists in every management decision. Dangers are there whether you choose passivity or action. The major lessons from debunking the "not risking is not risking" myth may be twofold: first, passive risk taking is far more costly, negligent, and irresponsible than commonly believed; second, active risk taking is far more profitable, responsible, and protective than commonly believed.

Myth Number Two:
Sharing Risk Reduces Its Dangers

Expanding the pool of risk participants reduces your share of potential loss. This makes risking more bearable, even if it also diminishes your share of potential gain. But the myth is only half right in this respect; although risk sharing disperses danger more broadly, it completely fails to reduce the total amount of potential loss. Spreading the components of a risk simply rearranges and reallocates its dangers among several parties.

Risk sharing serves managers' political, bureaucratic, and partisan interests in both legitimate and questionable ways. On the questionable side, the more parties participating in your risk venture, the less your own culpability and liability. When used cynically, this risk tactic can amount to pooled cowardice and prepurchased finger pointing. Risk-sharing tactics, used unethically, can entrap unwary parties by concealing the maximum costs of the risk.

Used openly, spreading risk around divides the total danger into smaller, more affordable, and presumably equal amounts. In practice, however, risk-sharing parties seldom bear the costs of these dangers equally. Consider the distribution of risk penalties for Ford Motor Company's mistake involving the location of the Pinto's gas tank: "The exposure to risk was very different for the executives who approved the design, Ford which had to pay the lawsuits, and the consumers who were injured or died" (MacCrimmon and Wehrung, 1986, p. 14).

Risk sharing works fine, for instance, in large-scale management risks, multi-million-dollar technology research and development ventures. The tactic backfires, however, when the risk of loss is spread around within the same company or passed on to innocent parties, like fellow managers, suppliers, or customers. What the individual leader or unit gains by spreading risk around, the overall organization loses.

When used for more commendable purposes, risk sharing makes it possible to take risks that might otherwise never be considered or implemented, such as expensive research and development projects. It also permits management risks during recessionary times and in other risk-averse circumstances. When used ethically, risk sharing expands support and strengthens buy-in for taking one of the most difficult of all risks for a manager: a risk that offers high gain and threatens high loss.

Myth Number Three: Risking Is Gambling

In *The Devil's Dictionary*, Ambrose Bierce wrote: "The gambling known as business looks with austere disfavor on the business known as gambling." Though ordinarily viewed as much the same thing, management risking and professional gambling differ in four ways.

First, gamblers display different risk-related psychological traits. For example, they habitually take chances and allow the urge to gamble to take precedence over all other interests. They take risks just for the thrill of it and seldom learn from risk failures (Bergler, cited in Singh, 1970). Moreover, gamblers are fully content with victories won by luck, while managers search for situations in which they play a key role in achieving their goals.

Second, society places a higher social value on calculated management risks than on the random, roulette-wheel risks of gamblers. "Society," suggest two management authors, "values risk taking but not gambling, and what is meant by gambling is risk taking that turns out badly" (March and Shapira, 1987, p. 1413). Failed management risks at least test ideas in beneficial ways. Gambling does not: "A true gamble does not test a refutable principle, but merely tries a random chance. Therefore, it cannot produce valuable knowledge" (Gilder, 1984, p. 252).

Third, precise and statistically proven laws of probability determine how chance operates with gambling. The odds of losing your bet on an American roulette table, for instance, are about 97.4 percent (MacCrimmon and Wehrung, 1986). In management, uncertainties can never be predicted or prevented. They can only be anticipated and diminished.

Fourth, gambling risks occur in an entertainment environment, can be addictive, and are based on win/ lose rules only. None of these necessarily apply to management risking.

Professional gamblers and managers do, however, share one significant risk-taking behavior: risk-taking caution. Full-time, working gamblers, for example, take gambling risks far more carefully than generally presumed. For these gamblers and managers, research shows that the more they know about their risk, the more cautious they become (Philips, as cited in Dickson, 1981).

In addition to both being "games" involving rules, luck, and skill, gambling and management risk taking have a practical similarity: both require the systematic weighing of risks against rewards. This may explain why many successful business people enjoy card games from bridge to poker (Contavespi, 1990). Card games can teach many lessons about the psychology and strategy of risk taking, some of which may be applied to playing your hand at the management table.

John Werner Kluge, perhaps the richest man in America, has long used his interest in card gambling to develop his risk-taking instincts and style. He carries these risk skills over into his business and has for decades. Naturally, he believes in the generic, learn-by-doing lessons that games like poker can teach—lessons like developing an intuitive feel for "when to hold 'em and when to fold 'em." He believes the ability to gauge risks is crucial, for no one survives very long, he also contends, on luck or skill alone. And as for the fickle interventions of luck, what really counts, Kluge contends, is how you play your luck whether good or bad (Contavespi, 1990).

4

REFRAME YOUR PERCEPTIONS: AVOIDING THE DISTORTION FACTORS

Deciding to take a risk is an inside job. It happens mostly in our private, inner, mental world. A risk is a risk if you see it as one, no matter what anyone else claims. If it feels risky to you, then it counts as a true risk for you. Risk experts concur in acknowledging the subjectivity of risk perceptions. While we endeavor to address ourselves to *real* risks, we must recognize that this can only be done by tackling *perceived* risks. People have no alternative to reacting to situations *as they perceive them,* according to Rescher (1983).

How you perceive taking risks has an influence on your effectiveness in selecting and implementing them. Perceiving them more clearly enables you to react to them more calmly, pick them more mindfully, and manage them more competently. A precise understanding of risk perceptions supports greater mastery of risk taking.

No one sees a risk with twenty-twenty vision. The distortion in your risk "lens" is a function of your subjective attitude, and it shades your perception of the elements of each risk. A host of factors cause these distortions. Fear, ambition, pressure, circumstances, good and bad experiences—all color your risk-taking perceptions. Factors that push you toward a risk, like self-confidence, and factors that push you away from risk, like self-doubt, can distort your perceptions in harmful ways. Either factor can overstimulate your psychological reactions, resulting in unwise risk-taking decisions.

Just as you can change your glasses, so, too, can you grind and polish new risk perception lenses, correcting the accuracy of your vision. Risk vision problems are hardly, if ever, 100 percent correctable. However, even small corrections can improve your risk mastery noticeably. Seeing risks more discerningly improves every aspect of risk taking, from making the decision to handling ensuing dilemmas.

CHECK RISK
DISTORTION FACTORS

Like photosensitive sunglasses, your personalized risk lenses may or may not adjust your vision to current management conditions. From experience and habit, you look at them from a certain, natural angle. That angle defines how they appear to you.

Many managers have difficulty putting aside the barriers and worries that prevent them from taking risks. A relatively young manager, Ross Garber, the strategic planning manager for Epoch Systems, has noticed the tendency of many senior managers to see risk in mixed terms at best. That in itself, however, is not necessarily an undesirable habit. "My experience with senior management is that most of them realize the need to take risks and they want to take risks, but they don't know how to get from the place where they are, to the place where the risk could take them. As a result, it's much easier to just avoid the risk and stay where you are. Financial accountability pressures, for example, block much of management risk taking. Yet I see why risk taking is so difficult for managers. Barriers like the fear of the unknown, the hassles of being second-guessed from the sidelines, and the pressures of meeting revenue objectives or else" (Garber, 1992).

Risk researchers have pinpointed several ways risk perceptions, like those Garber observed, influence management risk decisions (Tversky and Kahneman, 1981). One way is by directing your attention to or magnifying certain features of a risk, like its loss penalties or its gain payoffs. If asked to lead a crucial but failing project, for example, you could focus so intently on its conspicuous problems that you overlook its unseen opportunities and pass up a career-advancing assignment. Perception also influences your risk decisions by excluding from view (and consideration) your full range of alternative choices, such as breaking a risk into smaller, more manageable chunks or stages. Your perceptions also sway your risk practices through your sense of responsibility for how a risk turns out. The more you see yourself as accountable for success, the more diligently you work to ensure the outcome.

Here are several guidelines to help you spot and adjust for distortions in your risk perceptions. Each involves uncovering your ingrained patterns of looking at risks—patterns that can warp and slant what you observe and determine what you overlook.

Check Your Risk Reactions

The more dramatic or dangerous a risk is assumed to be, the greater the inaccuracy of its perception. In everyday life, people consistently overestimate and underestimate certain kinds of risks, as compared to valid statistics on the same risks (Slovic, Fischhoff, and Lichtenstein, 1979). For example, people significantly overestimate the risks from accidents, tornadoes, pregnancy, floods, and cancer to their own personal health and safety. Yet they significantly underestimate the health and safety risks posed by smallpox vaccinations, diabetes, lightning, stroke, asthma, and other dangers.

The same risk misperceptions plague the management world. Managers talk about the possibility of being fired as a deterrent to taking risks. In reality, political or personality conflicts cause most firings. Little evidence exists that getting fired is either the most frequent or the most disastrous outcome of taking management risks. The belief in the potential for catastrophe distorts managers' reactions to risk taking and colors their predisposition to accept or reject it without sufficient consideration.

Check Your Recent Risk Experiences

The management risk you took most recently is the freshest in your mind, as are those experiences marked by unusual success or failure. These vividly recalled risk experiences can shift your perception of a current risk toward undue optimism or pessimism. If your last major management risk showered you in acclaim, you may plunge more boldly into a new risk now. If your last major management risk drowned you in humiliation, you may find fifty reasons to avoid your next risk.

Too often, managers apply painfully learned lessons too rigidly. Like Mark Twain's cat, once they have accidentally been burned by sitting on a hot stove, they refuse to sit on any cold ones in the future.

Check Your Risk Attitudes

Risk-oriented and risk-averse managers see the same risks differently. Think of the task of championing a major improvement in personnel policies, for example. Risk-averse managers see more readily, and scrutinize more closely, the dangers of precedent, control, and cost. Managers open to risk see more readily the potential improvements in morale, performance, and productivity.

They agree with T. Scott Shamlin, vice president and general manager at Motorola, that being risk averse minimizes the probabilities of winning, not just those of losing (Shamlin, 1989).

Another example: in a bank holding company, managers who were more open to risk saw the company's performance goals as less challenging, while the more risk-averse managers saw them as more challenging. The same corporate goals seen as highly ambitious by security-oriented managers were considered to be conservative by the risk takers, according to researchers (Grey and Gordon, 1978). Whether a risk appears more or less dangerous depends on the manager's personality, motivation, background, and sense of security.

Check Your Risk Values

You modify risk perceptions through the values you attach to your risk options. Risk researchers refer to your risk values as *utilities*. The seen or recognized utility of a risk strongly influences the perception of how dangerous a risk probably is, and has an impact on whether you choose to avoid or to take it. A utility provides a benchmark against which you compare the desirability or undesirability of a risk.

Your risk values influence the risks you take and your reasons for choosing them. If you value challenging long-established management practice, no matter how firmly entrenched, the attendant risk hazards will probably not deter you. As another example, if you value displaying visionary qualities, this could justify your taking leadership risks others might view as irrational or doomed to failure. Yet another example is preferring gradual over swift organizational changes, inclining you to select risks of the former kind and to reject those of the latter kind.

SHIFT YOUR RISK VIEWPOINT

Threatening dangers can shroud risk taking in darkness. It can be difficult to see dangers clearly, if at all. The darkness triggers your negative emotions, weakening your concentration and slackening your motivation. You focus on easily seen dangers, which hinders your effectiveness. Doing this undermines, overwhelms, and misleads you. You choose and reject management risks unwisely because of errors in perceiving less visible dangers.

It helps to view a risk from multiple observation points. Try looking at it from far away, from close up, and from the side. Examining a risk from several angles will create a more accurate picture; it adds depth and detail and increases the objectivity of your risk perception.

Changing risk perspectives requires only a shift in your point of view. As an aid to visualizing this shift, imagine looking at your risk with three types of optical lenses: a telescope, a microscope, and a periscope. Shifting your risk viewpoint, or "scoping your risk," means changing your mental picture in the same way a lens would.

View Your Risk Through a Telescope

Move to a more long-term view of your risk. Specifically, examine it in terms of an extended time frame. Does the balance of risk pros and cons change when viewed in relation to next quarter, next year, or several years from now? Do the risk penalties seem more bearable when spread out over a longer time frame?

Seeing your risk over long time periods allows a more detached view. How does your assessment change when the risk is viewed from the perspective of people affected by it, such as stockholders or other stakeholders? How do its hazards change when seen by a disinterested or detached party, such as a trusted colleague in another organization? With this added perspective, let your assessment incubate for a while, or at least for as long as urgency will allow.

View Your Risk Through a Microscope

Enlarge the smallest details of your risk—details that otherwise would be dismissed or overlooked. As we have all reminded each other now and then, genius in any undertaking lies in the details, if its success lies in the implementation. Zoom in on the micro-level elements of your risks, focusing on the dangerous or critical aspects, such as unseen cost overruns. You can also use this tactic to examine human relationship issues that involve all risk participants; such issues might include conflicting risk perceptions that could endanger the teamwork needed to implement the risk successfully.

View Your Risk Through a Periscope

Try something that is very difficult, but not entirely impossible: look around the "corners" of a risk. Try the following tactics: observe your risk from above (from the vantage point of managers more senior than you); observe your risk from below (from the vantage point of managers more junior than you); and observe your risk from indirect angles (from the vantage point of a supplier, a customer, or a competitor).

Applying an insight from Isaac Newton offers another way of seeing around the corners. He insisted he was able to "see further than others as a scientist" because he "stood on the shoulders of giants." He was, in other words, able to learn from knowledgeable experts. Find a giant in your risk area and stand on his or her shoulders. The higher vantage point that their expertise affords lets you see your risk from a broader perspective.

UPGRADE YOUR RISK MOTIVES

Two basic psychological drives reframe every risk perception to some extent. Achievement motivations focus mostly on the potential gains of taking risks. Avoidance motivations focus mostly on the potential losses of taking risks. Both motives influence whether one risk is seen as acceptable or unacceptable. Upgrading your motives involves adjusting your underlying reasons for taking risks. It involves examining your motivations. Are you only trying to avoid losses? Are you trying to achieve gains as well?

Avoidance motives are natural and customary tendencies to avoid feelings associated with risk-taking failure, such as regret and shame. Having a tendency to avoid the feelings that accompany risk-taking failure means you are probably motivated by avoidance. Hundreds of studies document how most people take risks primarily, if not exclusively, to hold on to what they currently possess. They readily and frequently take risks to prevent a significant loss in something they value, but not for the opposite reason: to create a significant gain in something they value.

These studies asked many types of people to make the same risk decision stated two different ways. One set of risk options emphasized what could be gained by risking; the other emphasized what could be lost. When confronted with these two options for the same risk, as many as 80 percent of the respondents would take a risk in order to prevent a large potential loss. They would not take it in order to create a large potential gain. The framing of the decision-making rationale as one of gains versus losses biased their risk-taking decision (Yates, 1992).

The influence of the way the goal or purpose of risking is framed, whether as avoiding loss or achieving gain, has been demonstrated in other studies. When given the choice of taking a small chance at losing five hundred dollars or incurring a definite loss of fifty dollars, most people opt to take a small risk with their five hundred dollars. But when people are given the option of "insuring" their five hundred dollars with a fifty-dollar "premium," most opted to pay the fifty, even though a premium is the same as a definite loss of fifty dollars (Fischhoff and others, 1981).

Risk experts explain our tendency to risk less often to pursue gains, but more often to avoid loss, as a "prospect theory." "In choosing among risky prospects, people will underweigh outcomes that are probable compared to outcomes that are certain. This tendency manifests itself as risk aversion in choices involving sure gains, and risk seeking in choices that involve sure losses" (Bowman, 1982, p. 35).

As applied by managers, the prospect theory may reflect a "come out even" attitude among managers and organizations. You may not gain, but at least you won't lose.

In contrast to these avoidance-aimed motives, achievement-aimed motives are natural and customary tendencies to seek feelings associated with risk-taking success, such as fulfillment, satisfaction, pride, elation, and so forth. The need to experience these feelings impels us to see and seek the potential gains from opting to take risks. Having a stronger tendency to want the feelings associated with risk-taking gains means you are probably motivated by achievement.

Specifically, you can upgrade your risk motives by putting equal, if not more, energy into seeing the potential gains from your risks as you would into avoiding their potential losses. It is not the case that one should be overlooked in favor of the other. The idea is to balance your perception of both sides of the coin. Consider the gains as well as the losses, giving both equal weight.

Worry less about getting the unwanted (losses) and

more about not getting the wanted (gains). In other words, concentrate less on how a risk could keep you where you are and concentrate more on how it could get you where you want to be.

Large profits and fast growth come more from achieving gains than from preventing loss. Yet just staying even and holding onto the status quo is what most managers "see" and "seek" when considering a risk choice.

In the absence of any proven rule of thumb, answer the following questions before risking to achieve gains. Would your organization's resources cover any loss from gain-driven management risk taking? Does your competitive environment respond quickly and profitably to risk gains, such as new or improved products and services? Does your business sector or strategy require slower, less risky rates of growth, or faster, more risky rates of growth?

CALIBRATE YOUR RISK RATINGS

Balancing how you look at a risk with how others regard it "calibrates" your risk. This broader risk perspective allows you to see your risks more objectively. What your risk vision distorts, for example, another's may correct. To calibrate your risk, you must measure your perspective against other standards and viewpoints. There are several ways you can calibrate your risk perspective and make it more accurate.

Use Industry Risk Ratings

Generate two lists: one of risks externally imposed on your business or industry, such as risks originating from your main competitor(s), and one of risks internally chosen by your firm or division, such as consolidating an operation from several to one location.

In creating a list of the top five or ten of each of these risks, ask a group of senior managers to write down their own lists without consulting anyone. This process could be expanded to include many others, such as suppliers and subordinates.

Call a meeting of a small group to create your combined list of top risks. Begin by merging the lists, eliminating duplicate items and rewriting them to add or clarify key aspects. Take time to make sure everyone understands and agrees with the distinctive meaning and scope of each item. Ask everyone to vote for the top one-third of all the items listed and rank all items in order of their number of votes.

In ranking your risks, here are some potential criteria for ranking your top externally imposed risks: (1) the average or expected likelihood of occurrence in the current business environment, (2) your degree of exposure to harm if it does occur, (3) the size of the potential negative impacts, and (4) the importance of the potential negative impacts, given current business priorities and problems.

You may want to develop two versions of your list, one for short-term and one for long-term risks. You may also find it useful to ask everyone to rank the final list another way: by the degree of control you have over each risk. Put at the top those risks over which you exercise the most influence or leverage. Finally, the list may have more practical value if it excludes the most obvious, enduring, and routine risks in your business or industry.

Use Organizational Risk Ratings

Calibrate your risk for your organization's current status. What trends, issues, or circumstances could significantly influence the outcome of your risk? If you are new to your unit, your boss, or your organization, take time to check out their attitudes and practices. One clear indication of your risk-taking culture is the stories people repeat about famous risk-taking episodes.

Use Career Risk Ratings

Calibrate each risk-taking choice from the vantage point of your current career plans and options. Leading the charge in a controversial management risk, like changing an already successful product or service, raises different issues in an early career stage than it does at mid-career. There are, for example, good reasons to consider taking more risks at the start and at the height of a career than conventional career strategies promote.

In calibrating your career risk ratings, ask yourself four questions. First, how does your professional status influence your risk perspective? (Does it deter you from taking even small risks?) Second, how does your career status enrich that perspective? (Does it help you see hidden risk dangers in a more clear-headed way?) Third, how does your status distort your management risk perspective? (Does it cause you to inflate your estimates of potential payoffs?) Fourth, what major career change has occurred since you rejected your last major management risk? (Does it justify reevaluating your perceptions of the risk, whether favorably or unfavorably?) Answering these questions keeps your career risk perspective more flexible and up to date.

APPLY TWO SIMPLE STATISTICAL LAWS

Two long-proven statistical laws can help you more accurately perceive the odds of your risk succeeding: the Law of Large Numbers and the Law of Independent

Events. Most managers see their risks in terms of misleading "rules of thumb" about the average chances of success. This can backfire in ways that could be prevented by realigning your risk perspective according to the two laws.

The Law of Large Numbers

The Law of Large Numbers sharpens your risk perceptions by reminding you of the limitations of using averages in judging risk outcomes. It prevents misapplying your industry's average success or failure rate to your specific risk. Knowing the reliable and normal average for anything requires lots of data. If you were estimating the number of cold calls necessary to make one large sale, for example, ten cold calls would give a highly inaccurate sales average compared to one hundred cold calls. (If you doubt this, see how long it takes to get an average of half heads and half tails in tossing a coin.) What the law means is that if your industry average of success with, say, a new product is three out of ten, you will reach that average only after developing a very large number of new products. The good news: the larger this number, the greater the chances of your results matching what you expected to get. Unless you develop a very large number of new products under the same conditions, your industry success average will not apply. Unless there are a large number of new products (that is, a large number of statistical "events"), the average odds of success versus failure are more likely to be wrong than right.

The law also cautions you about the limits of past experience in judging the likely success or failure of management risks. Past experience serves as a fully reliable guide to estimate risk odds only when the characteristics of the new risk match those of the conditions that generated the historical data. Since this is rarely the case, past risk data should be checked for their relevance to the present risk.

The Law of Independent Events

The Law of Independent Events prevents basing expectations of the next risk outcome on the outcome of the last risk. Managers often assume, for example, that a string of failures increases the odds of the next risk succeeding, or that numerous successes increase the odds of the next risk failing.

The law rescues you from two dangerous but common misperceptions. First, it warns you against assuming that risk outcomes "even out"—that risk success will follow risk failure, and vice versa. If your last sales campaign succeeded, for example, you may assume that this increases the chances of the next one failing. Second, it warns you against assuming that risk outcomes repeat themselves, or that success follows success and failure follows failure. Management "common sense" supports this belief. If giving a work associate a second chance to improve a key area of work performance proves successful, you are somewhat likely to think the next second-chance risk will work out, too. The memory of your most recent risk success or failure (and the latter most strongly) has an enormous psychological impact on how you manage the next risk. The still-fresh sting of failure can weaken your risk management confidence, thereby decreasing the chances of a future successful outcome. These various reactions and assumptions lead managers to misjudge the odds of risk success and failure.

View all of your future risks as independent of all of your past ones, if only in terms of the likelihood of success or failure. Their independence means each risk outcome results from a separate or independent set of conditions and premises. The success of your last new product, for example, has no statistical bearing on the chances of your next new product succeeding.

Psychologists have a "gambler's fallacy" theory explaining why we tend to ignore these two principles. This theory contends that we all have "a strong psychological tendency to impose order on the results of random processes, making them appear interpretable and predictable. We prefer to believe some universal law of ultimate fairness or statistical favoritism acts in roughly predictable ways to even-out risk taking success and failure. In reality, the predictability of future risk outcomes has nothing to do with past ones, assuming they are independent events" (Slovic, Fischhoff, and Lichtenstein, 1979, pp. 192–193).

RAISE YOUR
RISK WATERLINE

Another way of reframing your risk-taking perspective comes from the late Bill Gore (founder of W. L. Gore & Associates, maker of Gore-Tex and medical products) by way of Tom Peters (1987b). Gore compared the level of acceptable risk with the waterline on boat A in Figure 4.1. Any risk above that waterline was okay at his company. As the metaphor implies, the damage from risk taking above the waterline will not sink the boat, steer it off course, or otherwise impair its ability to deliver its goods to its destination. But incurring any risk holes below the waterline means getting prior approval from the management captain.

Gore's risk metaphor poses several practical problems for managers: if, when, how, and where to place the

Figure 4.1. Risk Waterlines.

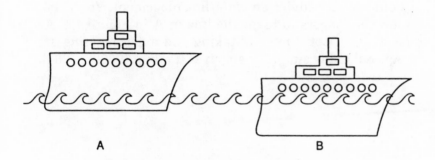

A   B

Source: Peters, 1987, p. 265. Used by permission.

waterline. Do you place it lower, as in A, or higher, as in B in Figure 4.1? In reality, of course, few managers actually determine so definitely or communicate so clearly the dividing line of unacceptable and acceptable risk taking. Neither do they adjust for rough and calm organizational seas. They probably assume everyone knows what is acceptable, a dangerous assumption in today's turbulent business environment.

Gore's metaphor, when applied with a touch of creativity, can help reframe perceptions of responsible risk taking in your work unit. Discuss it at a meeting of other managers and your staff, asking them to help define the risk waterline and determine when it should be raised and lowered. Literally draw a line and ask them to identify specific risks below it that could "sink the ship." Also ask them to indicate specific risks causing survivable damages, however costly.

You can also use it, as Tom Peters urges, as a tactic for increasing responsible risk taking by lowering the risk waterline. A lower waterline allows maximum experimentation and innovation without exposure to irreparable or unaffordable damages. Peters hesitates to provide exact advice on waterline placement. Yet he implores managers to favor the line in A in Figure 4.1. As he warns, "Constant risk-taking and experimenting are required today simply to survive" (Peters, 1987b, p. 264).

___

5

IMPROVE YOUR DECISION MAKING: TAKING THE RIGHT RISK AT THE RIGHT TIME

"The main goal of management science must be to enable business to take the right risk. Indeed, it must be to enable business to take greater risks—by providing knowledge and understanding of alternative risks and alternative expectations" (Drucker, 1985). Risk mastery requires judging when to initiate management risks— and when not to—without regretting the decision. The fact that all risks contain elements of uncertain danger and opportunity lends urgency and importance to the risk decision-making process.

The tactics discussed in this chapter will help you safeguard and strengthen your decision making. They include toughening your risk rationales, optimizing risk research, equalizing your reasoning and intuition, testing risk data, and asking the essential questions of risk taking.

TOUGHEN RISK-TAKING RATIONALES

Your harshest critics judge the astuteness of your risk choice using an oversimplified criterion: its final outcome. That judgment may be a humbling one for you unless the risk was well planned and thought out. Here are ways to inject more strength into your risk rationales.

Use a Risk Selection Checklist

A checklist can add a measure of "error proofing" to your risk justifications, helping you to assess their validity and thus avoid potential regret and retribution later on. Exercise 5.1 outlines a sample risk selection checklist for pretesting your risk rationales.

The risk selection checklist raises questions you must answer convincingly, for yourself as well as for risk allies and critics. The list is by no means exhaustive. (Some of these items are adapted from Toulmin, Rieke, and Janik, 1984). It might provoke a debate among risk participants—a debate that can be used as an alternative way to examine your risk reasoning. Through discussion, you can clarify, criticize, and rebut reasons for taking or not taking a risk.

Analyzing the soundness of your rationales in such ways helps to address two vital concerns. The first is whether your reasons link together to form a coherent decision-making justification. The second is whether, overall, you are on the right track and headed in the right direction. Considering the following additional risk "argumentation" questions will further sharpen the soundness of your risk decisions.

- What claims or assertions are you making in your decision to risk (claims, for example, about not needing additional funds for the risk)?

- How confident are you in your estimate of the chances of your risk succeeding?

- How adequately do your risk-taking reasons support your decision?

Exercise 5.1. Risk Selection Checklist.

Rate each item from 1 (lowest) to 5 (highest) depending on the extent to which it bolsters your risk decision. For the "anticipated profits" criterion, for example, the higher its numerical ranking, the more it serves as support for your decision. (Always consider these numerical ratings as estimates, not as statistically significant numbers.) Create your own checklist, put it in writing, and have it reviewed and updated periodically.

		Lowest			Highest	
1.	Anticipated profits	1	2	3	4	5
2.	Success odds	1	2	3	4	5
3.	Confidence in success odds estimate	1	2	3	4	5
4.	Management control over dangers	1	2	3	4	5
5.	Measurability of success payoffs	1	2	3	4	5
6.	Likely total losses of not risking	1	2	3	4	5
7.	Affordability of failure penalties	1	2	3	4	5
8.	Likely intangible gains	1	2	3	4	5
9.	Breadth of risk commitment	1	2	3	4	5
10.	Depth of risk commitment	1	2	3	4	5
11.	Strategic importance of future needs or wants	1	2	3	4	5
12.	Availability of sufficient resources	1	2	3	4	5

Source: Highwire Management by Gene Calvert. Copyright © 1993 by Jossey-Bass Publishers. Permission to reproduce and distribute material (with copyright notice visible) is hereby granted. If material is to be used in a compilation to be sold for profit, please contact the publisher for permission.

- Do your risk-taking reasons connect and reinforce each other (or do they contradict and weaken each other)?

- Are your risk-taking rationales and claimed benefits ambiguous or unclear?

- What are the specific grounds for your risk taking decision? (Statistical data? Knowledge or expertise? Convictions or opinions? Experience? Observation? Other grounds?)

- How solid and reliable are the grounds for your decision?

- How should your decision be modified in light of limitations in information about the risk's true dangers or costs?

- What unwarranted assumptions, unconsidered circumstances, or unexpected changes could undermine your decision?

- How likely is it that any unexpected changes will occur, and what can you do to prevent them from causing your risk to fail?

In auditing your risk-taking reasons, also reexamine your motives. Reasons explain why your risk seems feasible and appropriate. Motives reflect your hopes, intentions, and desires in taking the risk. Motives often overrule reasons. You want to believe, of course, that your actions will indeed achieve desired outcomes, and this may color your judgment. Ask yourself, Have I mixed my risk-taking motives with my risk-taking reasons?

Adapt the Scientific Method

You do not have to be a scientist to modify the scientific method to improve your decision-making procedures. A skilled proponent of this technique is Richard Lesher, president of the U.S. Chamber of Commerce. The Chamber is America's largest business advocacy federation, with more than 215,000 member organizations and companies. Here is how Lesher uses a simplified scientific approach to making risk decisions:

When I have the time, I use a simplified version of the scientific method in deciding whether or not to take a major risk. In an informal but fairly rigorous way, I go through five steps. First, I research my risk. Second, I develop alternative ways to implement it. Third, I pretest the alternatives through debate or small-scale pilot tests. Fourth, I evaluate what I've learned about the pros and cons of the risk. And fifth, I do "reduction to practice," or build a working, prototype model to give my risk plan some real-world testing. If I have the option, I then conduct another mock-up test before committing a lot of resources to any major risk venture.

By the time I'm finished with these steps, I usually feel pretty confident about what is the best decision for me and my organization to make. I also feel confident, if I indeed choose to risk, about how to make it work, despite unresolved and unforeseen problems. My model has worked pretty well for me over the years. It keeps me from shooting from the hip. It limits my risks. And it usually puts me on the right side of risky decisions [Lesher, 1992].

Obtain Statistical Interpretations

A group of nationally respected social scientists concluded that risk assessments by most professionals, including business executives, lack statistical rigor and precision (Committee on Risk and Decision Making, 1982). Managers face complex decisions daily, but with statistically unverified and untested data. Even with access to the right type and amount of data, few managers possess the statistical skills to make sophisticated use of such data. They also lack the time to properly review it, especially when overloaded with data.

One answer, says the Committee, is to assess the prevalence of unwanted uncertainties. Translation: First, find qualified researchers capable of interpreting statistical concepts, like "probability distributions," into business English; second, assign them the task of collecting and analyzing data that will add to the number and quality of your decision-making resources; third, ask them to identify factors (or "variables") that have the greatest influence on (or "statistical correlation" with) risk success and failure; and fourth, have them explain the strengths and weaknesses of their data, such as the likely margin of error. Fifth, adjust the statistical conclusions with your own management judgments.

OPTIMIZE RISK RESEARCH

Streamline risk research and analysis by not searching for every possible solution. Set and enforce a reasonable limit to your research. As a practical guideline, you have reached a reasonable limit when you have analyzed all of the major risk components. The minor ones pose little danger to you. Concentrate on elements of your risk that will have the greatest influence on its success or failure.

There are several ways to counter the temptation to prolong the search for solutions: (1) compensate for the need to choose swiftly by choosing as wisely as you can; (2) compare the value of *more* analysis with the value of *better* analysis; (3) integrate your objective, data-based assessment with your subjective, analysis-based evaluation as a final research step.

Data will never completely relieve you from having to make difficult risk decisions. Overly persistent attempts to turn essentially qualitative risk components into quantifiable data tend to waste resources and delay inevitable judgments. No matter how accurate and conclusive your risk data, balance them with your own experience. Rely on your good perceptions more than stacks of the most scientifically sound data.

Stay alert for the point where your risk research is no longer productive, then force yourself to stop. Little will be gained from continuing to compile information that will not be used in any constructive way; you will succeed only in postponing your risk.

Learning more about factors that cannot be controlled does not reduce risk. It wastes time and resources, and it can immobilize and demoralize would-be risk takers. Part of learning to take risks is discovering the disadvantages of excessive knowledge—even in the Age of Information.

EQUALIZE REASON AND INTUITION

The American philosopher Ralph Waldo Emerson described intuition a century ago as "primary wisdom," a "deep force," and "the last fact behind which analysis cannot go" (Emerson, 1983, p. 269). Contemporary thinking views it as neither witchcraft nor wizardry, but as "simply a manifestation of a perfectly ordinary mental experience: That of knowing something without knowing how one knows it" (Gunther, 1985, p. 121). Rowan likens it to "knowledge gained without rational thought through years of learning and experience into an instantaneous flash" (1986, pp. 11–12). Others describe it as "a computer in which all of your native talents and specific and general knowledge are stored" (Hanson, 1977).

Exploit Intuition's Risk Relevance
Increasingly, researchers, business professors, and managers alike are recognizing the legitimacy and value of intuition as a functional "sixth sense" in decision making. Intuition and its relative, instinct, compensate for some of the limitations of logical and rational thinking in making risk decisions.

It makes good sense for managers to embrace an intuitive approach to decision making. The turbulent times in which we now live require all of us to rely more on our instincts. Confidence in rational analysis has been shaken by turmoil in the surrounding environment rather than by weakness in the logic being applied. To the extent that logical solutions become inadequate, the manager of the future will have to rely even more on intuition than he or she does today, according to Roy Rowan in *The Intuitive Manager* (1986).

Rowan describes the role of intuition in two enormously successful, but risky, decisions. One involved the initial purchase that created one of America's largest franchise chains, and the other involved the publication of a best-selling book.

In the first example, Ray Kroc took the risk of buying out the McDonald brothers for a then-exorbitant $2.7 million (against his lawyer's advice) because his instincts kept egging him on. McDonald's became a Cinderella story of growth and profits, earning billions in profit for Ray Kroc and his investors.

In the second case, editor Eleanor Friede followed her intuition by publishing a manuscript already turned down by two dozen publishers. Her own marketing department scaled the first printing down to ten thousand copies. *Jonathan Livingston Seagull* eventually sold over 10.2 million units. It made millions for Macmillan because Eleanor Friede acted on her hunch.

Managers of small, entrepreneurial businesses rely on their intuition fairly regularly. A large survey revealed that while about half of them "consult facts, trends, and resources most or all of the time," one-fourth rely on intuition. When a risk clashes with conventional wisdom, however, nearly half of those surveyed "still follow their intuition at least half of the time" (Pollock and Pollock, 1986, p. 24).

Augment Rational with Intuitive Analysis

In contrast to intuitive approaches, rational analysis imposes a systematic and organized pattern on risk decision making. It structures decisions with logic, data, and experience. It gives order to ill-defined issues, shifting conditions, and fuzzy outcomes. It involves steps that are well known to managers, such as evaluating the risk problem, its alternatives, and its environment. And it uses a range of methods, from informal brainstorming sessions to marketing research to advanced statistical tools.

Intuitive instincts enhance decision making by moving personal relevance to a higher rank in the hierarchy of elements to consider. Unfettered intuition bolsters your risk-taking initiative and imagination. Intuition inspires you to reconfigure, reshape, and remold your concerns and alternatives. Just as advantageously, intuition questions hasty or otherwise irresponsible decisions. The most effective strategies for risk decision making combine aspects of both rational analysis and intuition, with the latter becoming increasingly important.

Consider how far into an unpredictable future the consequences of each decision extend. The further the extension, the less you need to rely on logic and the more you need to rely on intuition. The higher up you go in the management hierarchy, the further the outcome of decision making will extend. Consequently, the higher you move up as a manager, the more you need to develop your intuition in making risk choices.

Query Risk Hunches

Rowan (1986) offers four ways to test your intuitive risk hunches. First, find out whether the facts support your instincts. Ask the market researchers, number crunchers, and consultants to contest or confirm your proposition.

Do what you can to eliminate your most nagging uncertainties. Second, be prepared to back down. Instead of clinging stubbornly to an idea, exercise your option to switch directions, right up to the last minute. Third, describe your hunch to people you trust who can bring their expertise to the decision-making process. These friendly critics may find flaws that intuition is causing you to overlook. And fourth, test-market your risk hunches; carry out small-scale, affordable tests whenever possible. Do as much "reconnaissance" of the marketplace as you can.

Use Intuition Your Way

Rid yourself of the notion of some special or complicated formula for mixing reason with intuition in the decision-making process. Each manager finds his or her own way to use instinct with their rationales. That is how successful entrepreneur and CEO Laura Henderson managed the steady growth of her consulting firm over a dozen years.

> The biggest risk I take is managing my own way. A lot of what I've done contradicts popular management thinking. To manage this organization well, I needed to manage in a way consistent with who I am. A lot of people told me I didn't know what I was doing while developing this company into a leader in its industry. And guess what . . . they were right!
>
> Often I learned what to do only after, not before, making a risky decision. When you're truly an entrepreneur, you don't always know what you're doing. If you're willing to make mistakes doing it "your way" and learning from them, then I say, go for it!
>
> Female managers are often encouraged to go against their own basic management instincts and manage in a way of sync with who they are and what they want to achieve. I think it's a necessity,

and an obligation, for all managers to go with their intuition and manage the way that works best for them. It's not easy, but it's worth it in the long term [Henderson, 1992].

"Seeing" decisions in new, intuitive ways requires some flirtation with absurdity and humiliation, observes psychiatrist Abraham Zalesnick of the Harvard Business School (Rowan, 1986). In a managerial environment that values rational solutions, it requires courage to believe that saying "I feel" is just as valid as saying "I think" in making risk decisions. But even given the risks, managers at all levels acknowledge the value of using intuition as an additional tool for making tough choices.

TEST RISK DATA

You cannot control the availability or reliability of the information you need when planning for decisions. Steps can be taken, however, to prevent misinterpreting or misusing it.

First, avoid becoming addicted to data. Infatuation and preoccupation with data analysis lead normally savvy managers to foolish decisions. For example, much research went into the development of the Ford Edsel, but it still flopped.

Second, verify your data. How scientifically were they collected? Do other data confirm or contradict them? What is the margin of probable error? Any researcher or statistician can help you assess the strengths and weaknesses of your data for your decision-making purposes.

Data, that is, "the facts," never speak for themselves. We speak for them, and when we do, we contaminate the data's presumed objectivity with our natural subjectivity. Answering the following questions will alert you to the possible weakness of data and to the potential for misapplication of them.

- Am I defending my decision primarily because "the data support it"?

- Am I inflating my level of confidence in the risk choice because "the data support it"?

- Am I justifying the costs (whether in people, dollars, time, or information technology) of getting more data because I'm afraid to make a tough decision?

- Am I confident in the people who collected the data? How impressed am I with their qualifications?

- How much confidence do I have in the methods used to obtain the data? How likely is it that the research methods could produce misleading information?

- Am I satisfied with the appropriateness of the materials or people from whom the data were collected? How similar are these materials or people (for example, the people interviewed, the equipment tested, or the firms studied) to those involved in my risk decision?

- How much confidence do I have in the interpretations made or conclusions reached from the data? Do the interpretations make sense, even if they differ from my own experience?

- Have I expended a reasonable and appropriate amount of time in finding and using all needed data?

- Will additional data change my mind about my risk? Will additional data justify their cost?

Test for other sources of contamination in your data, such as fears that might cause you to over- or underestimate the reliability of your information, or pressures from work associates that could cause you to give too much or too little attention to either the positive or negative implications of your information.

ASK THE ESSENTIAL QUESTIONS

There are four essential questions to answer for every risk decision. Each probes one of the four basic elements of any risk: uncertainty, gain consequences, loss consequences, and significance (Siegelman, 1983). By answering the questions, you will enhance the completeness and stringency of your decision; you will understand fully and measure more exactly the challenges facing you in implementing your decision. At a minimum, you will cover the core considerations of a well-made risk decision. And if you answer the questions again during each implementation step, you will also ensure maximum alertness and readiness to react to changes in the uncertainties, gains, losses, and significance of your risk.

Accept the Uncertainties

Ask yourself whether you can accept the uncertainties— the unknowns of risk taking. Uncertainties include three types of risk-taking unknowns: those uncertainties you know, those uncertainties you do not know, and those uncertainties you do not and can never know you do not know. Uncertainties inhabit all true risks. They also inhibit risk taking by hampering analysis.

You must, however, take risks in spite of unspecifiable outcomes. Taking risks requires accepting their many uncertainties. One cross-cultural study defined "uncertainty avoidance" as "the extent to which people

are comfortable with ambiguous situations or the unknown future" (Burnside, 1989, p. 4). For many
managers, accepting them seems an unnatural act.
Avoiding them is a far more instinctive reaction.

Know the Potential Gains

Ask yourself whether the potential gains justify your
risk decision. Gain consequences motivate all risk taking, whether done by an individual or an organization.
Each gain has time dimensions, from short-term to long-
term, as well as payoff dimensions, from large-scale to
small-scale. The various benefit possibilities justify
management risk taking. They also make up its purpose.

Determine as explicitly as you can how you and
your organization will benefit from the potential successes. This information will help measure risk achievements and sustain motivation to overcome discouraging
implementation problems.

Know the Potential Losses

Ask yourself whether you and your organization can
afford the greatest losses that may result from the risk
decision. Then consider your options for influencing their
occurrence, magnitude, duration, and consequences. Compare these estimated damages to the equally likely ones
of alternative risks, as well as those of not risking at all.
In addition, gauge the secondary fallout effects of your
losses, such as financial, political, technological, and
organizational.

With regard to these loss impacts, reflect carefully
on the psychological, family, and career damages of all
losses for you personally, such as their affordability and
acceptability: Will they be expensive and intolerable,
like losing your position or jeopardizing your marriage?
Or will they be inexpensive and tolerable, like a harsh
tongue lashing or feeling temporarily depressed?

Generally, we are most aware of losses activated by our own actions. Knowing this, we restrain ourselves from risking. The greater the focus on loss, the less likely the chances of risk taking (Dickson, 1981). It is important to know whether your fear of loss is causing you to avoid risk. Is your fear an instinctive reaction that you can control? Or is the potential loss so great that you should not be risking?

Weigh two key aspects of any risk as exactly as possible: the severity and frequency of loss. Severity is the amount of damage the loss causes; frequency is how often the losses occur (Athearn, Pritchett, and Schmit, 1989). For a manager, for instance, severity could be the amount of decline in profits from deciding to temporarily discount a product or service, while frequency is simply how often this risk tactic is used in the time period applicable to it.

Figure 5.1 compares logical evaluations of different severity-frequency combinations and provides a supple-

Figure 5.1. Evaluation of Loss Severity-Frequency Levels.

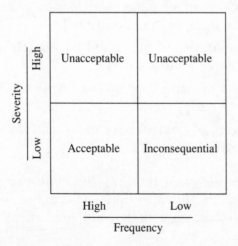

Source: Adapted from Ahearn, Pritchett, and Schmit, 1989, p. 24. Used by permission.

mentary risk decision-making tool. The process of criti-
cally assessing the severity and frequency of your risk
clarifies important decision-making factors. These primarily include negative aspects of the risk, such as
whether its injurious effects lean toward mildly delete-
rious or seriously destructive.

Bear in mind, however, that circumstances may justify a decision quite different from that suggested by the
cell in which your risk belongs. In a prolonged recession,
for instance, a high-frequency/high-severity risk may be
unacceptable, yet sensible if economic or other conditions make alternative decisions even less acceptable. In
other words, these risk evaluation categories offer
further considerations to improve the rigor of your risk
decision-making methods.

Be sure to probe each of these five critical aspects
of your potential risk-taking gains and losses:

1.   The scale of risk gains and losses. (How limited or
     unlimited are they?)

2.   The time span of gains and losses. (Are they of
     short, medium, or long duration?)

3.   The permanence of gains and losses. (How revers-
     ible or irreversible are they?)

4.   The costs of gains and losses. (Are they low, me-
     dium, or high?)

5.   The degree of control over gains and losses. (Is it
     low, medium, or high?)

Measure or guess these as best you can for your
specific situation. However imprecise your answers, this
exercise will help you make and implement sounder
decisions.

The definitions and measures of these gain and loss
categories must be set in the real-world context of each

risk. The short-term time span of a risk gain or loss
could be a few months with a vendor selection risk or a
year or more with a personnel selection risk; a low cost
for a new technology in the aerospace industry may
differ significantly from that in the banking industry.

Determine the Significance

Ask yourself whether you fully understand the significance of your risk. Significance poses the final, most
critical test of any risk decision. Determining the significance of any risk involves putting your own spin of
importance on it. How much does this risk mean? How
consequential is this risk? What is the priority of this
risk compared to others? How relevant is it to other
needs and goals? To whom does this risk impose the
greatest significance? Significance is a subjective element that balances the other more objective aspects of
management risk taking. The uncertainties, gains, and
losses must have meaning, must have importance, and
must have relevance to satisfy all the conditions of objectively defined management risk taking.

REACT TO RISK

Much of risk decision making involves analyzing possible alternatives and attempting to modify the risk before
having to make a final decision. Figure 5.2 illustrates
this process. Your actions for each of the five steps in
this model form the acronym REACT (Recognize, Evaluate, Adjust, Choose, and Track).

The REACT model could be used, for example, in
the process of bidding for a contract to sell your services
or products to a government agency (MacCrimmon and
Wehrung, 1986). You may have learned of this opportunity through the grapevine or seen a Request for Pro-

Figure 5.2. REACT Model of Managing Risk.

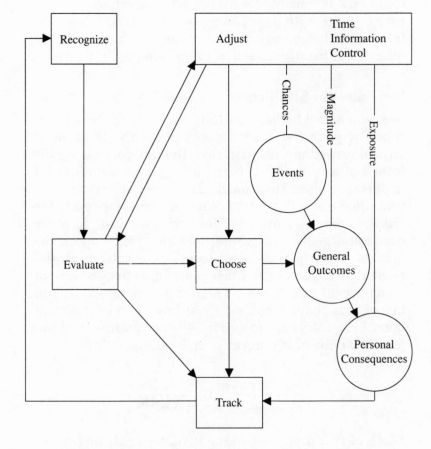

Source: MacCrimmon and Wehrung, 1986. p. 31. Used by permission.

posals (RFP) in a government publication. Your first step is to recognize that risk exists and has relevance for you.

The next step is to evaluate the risk. On the one hand, the profit margins may be smaller than normal and the billing process slow and cumbersome, making the risk unattractive. On the other hand, eventual payment is certain and the profit margins guaranteed. These are just some of the aspects you would evaluate. If the evaluation uncovers unacceptable facets of the risk, but countervailing reasons exist for taking it anyway, the intelligent risk taker then tries to restructure the risk.

The adjustment phase is next. It comes easily to managers who actively seek risks, but not so easily to those who actively shun them. The most basic risk dimensions to adjust are time, information, and control.

Table 5.1. Risk Phases and Risk Assessment.

Phases of Risk Assessment Process	*Components of Risk*		
	Magnitude of Potential Loss	*Chances of Potential Loss*	*Exposure to Potential Loss*
Recognize risks	What losses are possible?	What are the sources of uncertainty?	What is exposed to potential loss and to what extent?
Evaluate risks	Are the possible losses bearable and worth assuming?	Are the changes worth taking?	Is the exposure acceptable?
Adjust risks			
Gain control	How can potential losses be moderated?	How can uncertain events be prevented or made less likely?	How can risks be shared or spread?
Gain information	How much can I lose?	How likely is the potential loss?	Are options available for spreading risk?
Gain time	Can delay reduce loss?	Can delay reduce uncertainty?	Can delay reduce exposure?

Source: MacCrimmon and Wehrung, 1986, p. 28. Used by permission of Free Press and the authors.

You could gain time by forming a proposal team early and editing current boilerplate information instead of writing it from scratch. You could gain information by requesting copies of previous winning proposals from the agency and comparing your firm's costs and resources with those of the previous winning bidders. And you could gain control by submitting questions in writing whose answers would enable you to prepare a more competitive proposal, or by offering alternative, mutually advantageous ways of meeting the government's needs as the buyer and yours as the seller.

The next step is to choose a course of action. This is where your framing of the risk is crucial. You can only choose from options you see. If you decide to bid for the contract, you continue to evaluate and adjust the risk, tracking changes in the magnitude of potential losses and your chances of exposure to them. Table 5.1 lists some of the key questions management must ask for each of the key components of risk at each phase of the risk assessment process.

6

CONFRONT YOUR EMOTIONS: HANDLING THE ROLLER COASTER RIDES

Risk taking catapults you into a psychological zone of extreme shifts in mood and feeling. It bounces you back and forth between excitement and gloom, confidence and panic, pride and remorse. If warp-speed emotional roller coaster rides strike you as inconsequential, realize this: managing risk with effectiveness depends on passing its intellectual and psychological tests with equally high marks. Being prepared psychologically is as essential to initiating a risk as being prepared technically.

There are a number of techniques you can use to control the tension, steel yourself for unexpected blows and disappointments, and handle the emotional highs and lows at every phase of risking. This is the intimidating side of the problem for most managers. Yet learning to take risks responsibly involves learning how to successfully defuse emotional land mines. The following tactics will help you find alternate ways to pass safely through those mine fields.

LEARN FROM YOUR EMOTIONS

One tactic is to examine and reexamine your emotional reactions before and after taking management risks. The

101

strategy is to be an active learner in an area least acknowledged by many managers—that of the emotional management of risk. This tactic focuses on learning psychological lessons from your experiences. It urges you to reclaim the most powerful of all risk mastery insights: those of the emotional realm.

Detect Risk Emotions

Stay in tune with how you feel personally about your risk at each stage of the journey. Notice the risk-related feelings you would never tell other managers about. Those are the feelings most likely to influence your tactical management of the risk.

Emotional highs and lows are a hallmark of the risk-taking process, regardless of whether you accept or deny them. Your feelings change with the dips and curves of changing events. They may even come at you simultaneously: you have mixed emotions; you feel ambivalent.

When negative emotions shift into high gear, you lose some of your ability to evaluate a risk objectively. If you become enraged, for example, after hearing information about one component of your risk, your perception of the overall condition of your venture may become distorted. You start to dwell on the potential consequences of failure.

The greater your emotional awareness, the more effectively you can manage your ups and downs. Anticipating emotional intrusions will buy time—time to prepare for the emotional shocks and surprises of walking the highwire. And when the walk ends, you'll be ready to retrieve and save all the hard-earned lessons from experience.

Reexamine Risk Emotions

Spend a few minutes remembering two major management risks you have taken. Choose them from among your experiences with office politics, personnel hiring, job changes, client relations, and departmental and budgetary risks. Ask yourself how you felt before, during, and after making your decision to take the risk. Ask yourself how you felt during the long intermediate stage of taking the risk itself. Think about how you felt when it looked as though your risk would either succeed or fail, and when it actually did.

Such times are characterized by doubt, despair, and frustration. Everything seems to fall apart, and no response seems to work. The risk loses its excitement; the experience becomes torturous. You wish you hadn't taken the risk. The period ends when you finally emerge from the darkness of the process into the light of resolution.

By probing the emotional experiences of past risks, you can develop your ability to respond more wisely the next time. Reexamine both the successful and unsuccessful ventures. The latter will often provide the most revealing insights.

Counter Risk Stress

In the emotionally traumatic throes of a major risk, management consultant Leeda Marting sometimes gets up at 4 A.M. and exercises, pays bills, cleans house, bakes muffins—anything that distracts her from worry and calms her down enough to go back to sleep. This never solves her risk-taking problem. But it does blunt the concerns that wear her down physically and mentally. Like most people, she also finds it helps to talk through her risk worries with close friends or colleagues (1993).

You probably already know fairly reliable ways to calm and control yourself emotionally at work, from doing exercise to talking to confidants. Many entrepreneurs keep from worrying by "monitoring things constantly." About one-fourth take their minds off their worries through other business or leisure activities, and about one in ten do not worry at all, according to a survey (Pollock and Pollock, 1986). But whatever works for you, use it to keep your composure while taking the wrenching twists and turns of the high-risk roller coaster.

VERIFY YOUR READINESS TO RISK

Readiness can make a crucial difference in your ability to cope emotionally with a risk-taking venture. With practice, you can learn to master the emotional trials that come with the commencement of a risk. Two ways to do this are testing for readiness and waiting for readiness.

To test for emotional readiness, ask the following question: What is it about risk that alarms or unsettles me? If answering that question leaves you in doubt of your emotional fitness to risk, ask the question again in another way: What is it about the risk that would have to change in order for me to feel comfortable about taking it? Consider whether you have any practical control over these changes. If so, how comprehensive and effectual is it? Making these changes is especially important if they concern you personally, as with their busting your normal boundaries or patterns of risk taking. Assuming you have sufficient control over changes blocking your risk-taking readiness, answer yet another question: Are you fully prepared to do all it takes to implement these changes? Are you, for example, willing to experience the stress, initiate the actions, invest the resources, and accept the tradeoffs these changes may require?

Waiting for readiness is more difficult. Pop psychology tricks will not make it easier. As frustrating as it may be, your emotional readiness has its own timetable. Just because you want to be ready does not mean that you are. The same is true when others want you to be ready. Resist being pressured into taking a risk before you are psychologically primed for it.

If you are not ready to risk, don't punish yourself for it. Even if it means you have to wait a while, stay true to your emotional timetable. Pay attention to your gut reactions. The time will come when you know, without any misgivings, you are emotionally ready to proceed.

A true story about waiting out emotional resistance may be instructive, even if it digresses momentarily from the subject of risk endurance tactics. It happened to a senior manager I know. We will call him Paul.

Paul wanted to switch from a job his friends said only a fool would quit. His aim was to resume working as an independent management trainer and consultant. That involved three emotionally threatening risks: giving up a rewarding and secure job; becoming self-employed again; and getting his first book written and published. The more Paul researched and thought about each of these risks, the more disheartened he became.

Paul vacillated between feeling smart because he had this fabulous job and feeling dumb for not pursuing lifetime goals. But he wasn't ready to take the plunge. He was too afraid, too ambivalent, and too concerned about how others would judge his actions.

Then a stroke of good luck offered Paul a way out: he was offered a half-time position with a large consulting firm. It would allow him to hold on to his savings and at the same time embark on a new career venture. This was as much of a risk as Paul was willing to take at the time.

But his seemingly prudent strategy—that of taking a half-time risk—failed to produce the results he wanted.

In fact, his new career slowed to a crawl. After one year, all he had to show were a few small contracts and rough drafts of three chapters of a new book. Paul needed to use all of his time, not just half, to write the book, relaunch his business, and ensure a semblance of quality in his personal life. Working half time delayed his writing and the growth of his business for over a year. He finally quit the half-time job and used (or "invested") his savings to finance the book and the business.

Paul's willingness to act then, but not before, had a lot to do with emotional readiness. Nothing magical happened. Nor did he do anything clever or courageous. What emerged without conscious thought or effort was an emotional preparedness to risk in the face of uncertain consequences.

As frequently happens with risk taking, Paul ended up gaining far more than he spent financially, despite his initial hesitation. During the delay, he developed a marketable expertise in continuous quality improvement. This became, and still is, a profitable primary source of revenue for him. Most of all, Paul developed a deeper respect and greater tolerance for the emotional obstacles facing any risk taker. In risking, Shakespeare said, "readiness is all."

MAINTAIN
RISK FLEXIBILITY

Daniel Kehrer (1989, p. 39) defines "high-flex" risk taking as "the ability to be flexible in risk, to adjust rapidly and snap back if conditions change, or do not meet expectations." One aspect of this is staying clear about your goal—what it was that justified the risk in the first place. Another aspect is adapting constructively to unexpected crises.

This tactic requires a broad view of risk taking. Don't automatically interpret an emergency as a message that failure is certain. Put your emotional energy into mapping out a clear plan of action. At the same time, the situation will be more bearable if you respond with maximum emotional composure. By "keeping your cool," you stay alert and able to apply your energy to shifting strategies. People who are poorly adjusted tend to hold onto their ineffective tactics, refusing or unable to maintain flexibility in riding the highs and lows of risk taking.

DIVIDE AND CONQUER RISK

Psychologist Ellen Siegelman (1983, pp. 129–147) outlines seven psychological stages of risk taking:

- Become aware of negative feelings.
- Recognize the need to change.
- Experience ambivalence.
- Reduce the risk through preparation.
- Let it rest— incubate your final move.
- Take the step—act on your decision.
- Evaluate the outcome.

Each stage encompasses a set of emotions and employs tactics for dealing with those emotions both positively and effectively. The stages outlined, and their accompanying emotions, vary from person to person and according to each situation.

By arranging the milestones of management risk taking into sequenced stages, you essentially divide them and conquer them emotionally (Siegelman, 1983). The stresses of taking risks become bearable when they are experienced separately. Focusing on one step at a time frees up your creativity and concentration. You can act on what you can most control: the challenge posed by a single risk-taking stage. The better you handle the current stage, the more problems you circumvent in subsequent stages.

Stage One: Notice Negative Feelings

Pay attention to any physical and psychological clues that may indicate a risk decision coming your way. You may experience, for example, an uncrystallized sense that something is wrong and may require actions you would prefer to avoid. These feelings tend to take a negative form, like apprehension and vulnerability. Instead of dismissing these vague, nonspecific feelings as a passing mood or excessive worrying, pay more attention to them. It could give you a head start on handling an actual risk.

Stage Two: Recognize the Need to Change

This stage resembles Stage One and may even happen simultaneously. The subtle difference is that at this stage you are beginning to sense the desirability of making a change of some kind. You start having wistful thoughts about how you would like things to be, or how things would be under different circumstances. Most likely, you keep your musing to yourself for protection against automatic rejection by others. You can profit from these private reflections by exploring them further.

Stage Three: Experience Ambivalence

At this stage self-questioning shifts from "Can I really?" to "I will." As soon as you decide to risk, some form of reality shock sets in. You may feel pulled between your inclination to stick with the status quo or interfere with it. You may, for example, waver between excitement and worry, between approach and avoidance, or between belief and doubt. The ominous prospect of risk-taking failure provokes sobering second thoughts.

The decision to risk can be the most anxiety-producing aspect of the entire process. Once it is in action, these anticipatory misgivings often fade. The ambivalence you feel in this stage helps you by eventually pointing you in the direction of risk pursuit or avoidance. Siegelman recommends preparing to risk emotionally by openly welcoming any ambivalent feelings about a risk.

Stage Four: Reduce the Risk Through Preparation

Seize as much control as you can over the predictable dangers in your risk. It is not cheating to reduce risk dangers to the maximum extent possible; responsible management risk takers never take risks rashly. Focus your attention on preventing your emotions, positive or negative, from interfering with your risk reduction work.

Skepticism about how little your risk can be reduced can weaken your effectiveness in taking what safety measures there are to take. Every effort in the area of risk reduction is important. It can end up making the difference between success and failure.

Stage Five: Let the Risk Rest

Give yourself a break at this stage. For the moment, put aside the risk-taking debate. If you initiate a risk with your mental, emotional, and physical batteries low, you will deprive yourself of reserves you may need later to cope with unexpected complications.

Over-preparation can endanger the risk just as much as under-preparation. In sports, for example, pushing a team into competitive action without any break beforehand guarantees some mistakes from pre-game practice fatigue alone. Take a rest from your risk preparation by concentrating on other management priorities before launching the endeavor.

This pause differs emphatically from procrastination in three ways. First, it is pausing as a conscious act of self-direction, not as an unconscious act of self-deception. Second, it means feeling deservedly good, not deservedly guilty, about the break. Third, it is waiting attentively, not mindlessly. Pausing at this stage involves a purposefulness in waiting quite unlike the purposelessness of procrastination.

Stage Six: Take the Plunge

Take the plunge and act at some point, despite your reluctance and reservations. True procrastination, not pausing, tempts seductively at this stage. Taking a risk always demands leaping into the darkness, no matter how familiar the risk itself. Surprises, accidents, breakdowns, and more, shadow risk takers at all times.

Taking the step, psychologically at least, involves walking onto the tightrope. You may experience a disorienting sense of mental and emotional vertigo before taking the first step. You may also feel a reassuring sense of anticipation and relief that it will finally happen. Inner doubts haunt everyone no matter how superbly managed the risk has been so far. At some point, you must move forward based on untested conviction. If not, you slow momentum, weaken control, and lose initiative.

Stage Seven: Evaluate the Outcome

Forego the inviting temptation to omit this last stage. If nothing else, evaluation provides time to recharge your batteries before tackling other crises competing for your attention. Insist on taking the time to evaluate your risk, both for yourself and for your work associates.

Skipping this last stage could cost you in the end. You could fail to profit fully from your risk-taking investment. You could lose some of the benefits of repeating in future risks what you did right this time. Or you could overlook the future risks that every present risk spins off.

Just as the anguish of defeat can rob you of priceless and expensive insights, so can the excitement of risk-taking victory. In the warm light of triumph, we remember our actions differently than in the cold darkness of failure. Use extra care and candor in evaluating highly successful risks. Remind yourself of the natural tendency to accept success far more unhesitatingly and uncritically than failure. Evaluating each stage of a risk endeavor enhances mastery by viewing the process as ongoing with few, if any, clear or final end points (Siegelman, 1983).

RISK WHAT YOU FEAR

Risk taking involves a subjective sense of danger that you must learn to overcome (Dauw, 1980). Danger triggers a variety of fears, such as the fear of exposure to personal and professional ridicule. All of us bring our own set of fears to the risk highwire. Whatever they may be, those fears can wreak havoc, immobilizing otherwise capable and responsible takers.

Managers with high standards of performance for themselves as well as associates are particularly vulnerable to the effects of fear. A perfectionist manager, observes organizational consultant Suzanne Sisson, "internalizes failure and believes that the source of failure comes from within the self. The results are brutal self-punishment and severe limitations on the kinds of risks taken. Risk taking opportunities are perceived as sources of anxiety instead of interesting, if not exciting, challenges" (Sisson, 1985, pp. 39–42).

Admit Your Fears

Hiding or denying your fears impairs your risk mastery in several ways: by causing you to avoid taking self-initiated, voluntary risks; by causing you to postpone taking mandated, involuntary risks serving your own or your organization's best interests; and by compromising your management effectiveness. Harboring your risk fears can also keep you from bailing out of the wrong risk at the right time.

Taking management risks makes you responsible for errors of commission and omission. The psychological impact of this gives life and energy to your fears. Risk author Dr. David Viscott (1977, p. 62) wrote: "Often a businessman cannot risk because he fears . . . making bad decisions that will prove him unfit. You can't evaluate a list of potential business gains honestly and act decisively if you believe any failure will reveal your incompetence." Fear of revealing feelings of insecurity and inferiority keeps many managers from taking risks.

Susan Jeffers's book, *Feel the Fear and Do It Anyway* (1987), offers a pragmatic approach to handling fears like those experienced when taking management risks. Following her principles of embracing your fears and learning from them may be the most effective way to endure these or any fears. This may give you a better chance of turning fear frustrations into fear fulcrums.

Grow from Your Fears

Fears, including those of risking, never go away as long as you are growing as a manager. Continuing to grow means continuing to risk. Endless personal and professional development is the nonnegotiable price of managerial excellence. Imagine what might be lost by your not being the best manager you can be. Can you or your organization ever afford that? So you will need to achieve, and as long as you choose professional growth, as long as you choose professional excellence, as long as you take necessary risks, you will be afraid of something.

If you wait for your fears to go away, you will wait forever. They will never disappear completely. Waiting for this impossibility is playing a no-win "when-then" game. *When* your fear goes away, *then* you will take the management risk you have been avoiding. "Any risk that is important for growth will continually reappear until it is settled. If it is not settled there will be no growth," wrote Dr. Viscott (p. 38). Fear goes away after, not before, you take the initiative to risk. Acknowledging your fears now, then enduring them through the risk-taking process, will lead to professional and personal growth and the reduction of fear in the future.

The against-the-grain career changes made by Jeanne Hollister, vice president of Aetna Life and Casualty, illustrate the process of taking risks first, then experiencing a decrease in the fear of risking. Jeanne's pattern of career growth is becoming the rule, not the exception, for most managers, or so predict many career development experts. These kinds of risks, whether taken by necessity or choice, are contemplated with fear by most managers. As Hollister's experiences demonstrate, surviving career changes means constant adjustment to the new and the uncomfortable.

> While I didn't plan it, I've bucked the standard career path in my industry several times. I was trained initially as a property/casualty actuary. But early on, I switched to life insurance work. Believe me, these two insurance sectors have vastly different work cultures. Another career risk I took was leaving the technical side of the insurance business early in my career for a newly created managerial

position. I then made another unconventional career move by taking a planning position working with managers more senior than myself. This taught me not to be afraid to get into business areas over my head at the time . . . as long as I could do reasonably good work from the start and learn quickly.

One of the biggest risks I've taken is moving from the business to the corporate side of the firm. I would be dealing directly with people four organizational layers above me. It was a scary move and I had a lot of fears about risking it; a few of them proved valid, but most of them groundless. Among my fears that came true: some of my colleagues criticizing me as a traitor for moving to the corporate side; being insufficiently knowledgeable about corporate-level aspects of my new work; and being caught in the middle of decisions advantageous for the corporation, but disadvantageous for one of the business units, or vice versa. I was able to maneuver around these negative risk-taking outcomes, however.

My greatest and most threatening fears never materialized: becoming labeled and stereotyped as a "corporate" person; burning my bridges with the business side because of corporate decisions in which I participated; getting stuck in the "black hole" of corporate work; failing to perform well in the job; discovering too late that the demands of the position would be greater than I could meet; and finding a job I wanted back on the business side. This risk was definitely worth the trade-offs it involved. I stayed in it about eighteen months and was offered yet another new position that opened up as a result of a restructuring [Hollister, 1992].

See Fear as Normal

Everyone experiences fear when they find themselves in unfamiliar territory. All sane and sensible managers feel fear when they take risks. But this fear does not always have to hamper the ability to go forward with new ventures. Two respected training consultants experienced fear while developing a controversial program for the Office of the Secretary of Defense. Their design involved risks, which made the consulting firm hiring them quite nervous. The firm's vice president was blunt in his unhappiness with the program and with their training design in particular. Yet the design eventually earned top reviews from the client, the consulting firm, and the training participants. "I've been afraid of failure most of my career," admitted one of the consultants. "There are few major achievements in my career that I wasn't scared silly about at the time." He said his most meaningful career accomplishments came from his biggest career risks, particularly the ones he feared taking the most. He even laughed about the fact that much of his career was spent being afraid. Comfort can be gained from the knowledge that fear is normal during times of risk or in pursuit of any ambition. The experience of the two consultants confirms the wise counsel of Susan Jeffers for all risk takers: "Feel the fear and do it anyway" (1987).

Pushing through fear is less frightening than passively enduring it. To linger in the cold but shielding cocoon of fear tempts any risk taker. Some managers spend an entire career inside it. But a day of reckoning awaits when they lose the strength to penetrate fear barriers, when managers who are less qualified move ahead of them, or when the brass rings begin to exceed their reach. Ironically, notes Jeffers, the cost and pain of staying within the protective cocoon of fear exceeds that of pushing through it: "People who refuse to take risks live with a feeling of dread that is far more severe than what they would feel if they took the risks necessary to make them less helpless—only they don't know it" (1987, p. 28).

UNTANGLE
RISK MOTIVATIONS

Separating your various motivations for taking a risk allays some of its emotional discomfort. A greater motivational awareness helps move you beyond self-imposed risk-taking limits, whether they are limits of size or frequency. The more a risk intimidates you, the more advantageous it is to understand your motivations for pursuing it.

Three basic factors motivate us to engage in risk-taking behavior: expectancy, incentives, and motives. *Expectancy* relates to the outcomes you anticipate. These are the favorable outcomes you want and believe will happen. The *incentive* is your risk benefit and the likelihood of getting it. An incentive can be anything interesting to you about the risk, such as "what can't be done." And the *motive* is your tendency to take or avoid risky actions (Atkinson, 1957). Motives are your normal preference or disposition to grapple with risk-associated difficulties and uncertainties. The combined force of all three factors determines the total strength of your motivation to either seek or avoid a risk.

In actual practice, how do these factors work? How would they weaken or strengthen, for example, your motivation to initiate a major reorganization of your unit? If you assumed the gains were important and likely to occur (expectancy), you would be more likely to reorganize. If the benefits of the reorganization appealed to you strongly enough (incentive), you would probably reorganize despite poor success odds. If you are generally risk averse (motive), you would probably look for reasons not to reorganize.

Analyzing the influence of these three factors on a specific risk helps you improve your management of it. Probing risk expectancy can ease risk-taking anxieties by identifying anticipated outcomes precipitating this emotion. Research documents, for example, that anxious people tend to set extremely high or low aspirations in risk-taking situations as a defensive, self-protecting maneuver (Arrow, 1982).

Verifying your incentives helps clarify particularly strong emotional resistance—or attraction—to a risk. First, scrutinize what interests you about it, such as meeting a crucial management goal or proving a long-held belief. Next, assess the risk-related difficulties of satisfying your interest. Finally, examine whether and how much this assessment will affect your feelings about the risk acceptability or unacceptability.

Investigating your motives sheds a stronger light on the firmness of your risk disposition–based reasons for pursuing or averting a risk. Which reasons spur you to take the risk? How pragmatic are they? And finally, are you hiding darker, less socially accepted risk-taking or risk avoidance motives from yourself or others?

Despite vigilance and the best of intentions, feelings and emotions intrude at all phases of the risk decision-making process, from how the risk decision is perceived or framed (as described in Chapter Four) to handling the psychological ups and downs of risk implementation. This chapter has presented a number of ways to handle this fact of management risk taking: choosing to learn and grow from your risk-taking emotions; respecting your current level of emotional readiness to risk; staying flexible in adapting to the emotional stretches your risk requires; focusing intently on the emotional and other challenges of the current risk stage; risking in spite of your ever-present fears; and finally, gaining an upper hand over your upsetting risk emotions by uncovering and defusing them. Having fastened your emotional seat belt for the risk-taking roller coaster, reducing the dangers of the risk is your next step toward risk maturity.

7

REDUCE THE DANGERS:
RISK TAKING IS NOT RISK FREE

Managers never completely eliminate risks, but they relentlessly try to minimize them. It often boils down to finding the best ways to reduce as many negative risk factors as possible on the lowest budget. Reducing risk dangers has both strategic and tactical benefits. Strategically, it strengthens the justification for taking the risk. Tactically, it minimizes ongoing hazards, while curtailing losses. On both levels, reducing the dangers means risking more responsibly.

On a psychological level, curtailing dangers makes risking less frightening and more comfortable. Generally, the smaller the danger, the greater the comfort. Eliminating or diminishing known dangers in advance, for example, affords you the time and energy to respond to unknown ones emerging unexpectedly along the way.

There are several ways to deal with the dangers in any risk (Carroll, 1984). You can choose a risk that is less dangerous or simply refuse to risk. Alternatively, you can reduce exposure to hazards by limiting the amount of time and money invested, or by creating backup options.

Long-time entrepreneur consultant Charlotte Taylor (1991) summarizes one of the essential skills of reducing risk danger: "Never limit yourself to doing 'business as usual' automatically. Don't get complacent or fixated with the status quo. Keep looking at the playing field, the players, and the game at all times. It's the only way to survive in business today."

Risk reduction tactics can be separated into three categories: avoiding danger, limiting danger, and spreading danger among several parties. If you persistently take (or avoid) big enough risks, sooner or later you will fail and face the consequent fallout. Whether your failure is on a huge scale, or at the other end of the continuum of risk penalties, one or all of these sets of tactics can help you survive them.

AVOID DANGER

Three basic methods of curtailing potential danger all involve good judgment about when to pass up a risk. Each tactic requires putting aside for the moment one of the arguments in Chapter One: that avoiding risks never gives you 100 percent immunity from negative consequences.

Choosing Not to Risk

The safest course is always not risking, according to conventional management wisdom. That view favors risk avoidance over risk taking as standard policy and practice. It argues that risk taking creates unnecessary hazards, that managers should skirt risks whenever practical, and that the same goals can usually be reached through safer strategies. "The corporate structure is intrinsically, not accidentally, a risk avoiding mechanism," observed futurist Joseph Coates (1979, p. 177).

The skill in using this tactic is knowing just what grounds justify risk aversion. It is not enough to assert that not risking offers a safer, wiser, or more responsible option. Our work environments require bullet-proof protection from instances when dismissed dangers from your decision *not* to risk actually come to pass. When the witch-hunting and scapegoating start, you'll need justi-fication for choosing not to risk as a danger aversion tactic.

You can defend yourself on a number of grounds. No one expects you, for example, to take actions that could result in a denied promotion. Nor are you expected to take risks whose benefits do not justify their costs. In addition, this may be the wrong time or place for the risk you choose not to take. Finally, no one requires you to pursue risks containing potentially devastating legal, and therefore financial, liabilities. (In a survey, 40 to 50 percent of CEOs said that the threat of legal liability caused them to discontinue or withhold new products [Silas, 1991]).

Abandoning a Risk

You have a right to walk away from any risk at any time in order to avoid its dangers. You resolve not to face ad-ditional or greater dangers and back your determination by simply abandoning the venture. This requires unusual management qualities: the private self-confidence and public self-control to walk away when others want to continue.

Risks have a tendency to generate their own mo-mentum. The more you have explained and defended your plan, the harder it becomes to dismantle it. Aban-doning your risk conflicts with your desire to be proven right about your planning skill and judgment. There will be less of a conflict if you identify your "walk away point" in advance of risking, just as you might when planning a major negotiation.

Richard Branson, founder and CEO of Virgin Records, warns against sticking with a risk when the dangers soar to unacceptable levels. In such circumstances, he considers it good management sense to cut your losses and get out. Another deal can always be found. "Deals are like London buses—there is always [another] one coming" (1985, p. 7). Sometimes the next deal turns out better than the one given up. At a minimum, cutting losses earlier, rather than later, frees you to exploit the next deal that is likely to emerge.

Branson used this tactic when he walked away from negotiations for a second Boeing 747 aircraft for his new airline. He wanted, but could live without, having another airplane. He showed a willingness to walk away by refusing bankers' demands for other parts of business holdings as security. Because of his firm resolve to "fold his hand" when necessary, he was able to say no to the bankers. He ended up getting the loan without increasing the financial dangers involved.

Planning Not to Risk

Proven methods of strategic planning can be used to preempt risk dangers. The most basic of these methods, a SWOT assessment of strengths, weaknesses, opportunities, and threats, not only targets your risk dangers but also implies ways to bypass them. Use the same strategic planning techniques to circumvent a risk-taking danger that you would employ to skirt any management danger. Examples include writing clear and measurable objectives; conducting a full, but reasonable and efficient, investigative search; developing contingency options for the most obvious and likely dangers; and forging strong and strategic links between your plan and your business values and vision. In other words, draw on your strategic planning experience and expertise to anticipate and reduce your risk dangers.

Planning not to risk pays many dividends. It helps

you completely sidestep some of the dangers (although nothing can protect you from all of them). It heightens your awareness of potential perils. And it enables you to zero in on the information most crucial to your success. As one management risk researcher concluded, "Most decision makers do not need more information, but rather the ability to process the information they have" (Blaylock, 1985, p. 219). Here again is where risk planning pays off: if you plan your research, you will more likely end up with the right amount of the right kind of information.

The following risk planning checklist poses some of the questions you need to answer regardless of whether you intend to avoid, limit, or share dangers.

Risk-taking goals:

- What is the primary purpose of taking this risk?
- What are the secondary purposes of taking this risk?
- What is the value of the goal to you, the firm, and other key parties?
- How will you and other key parties measure goal achievement, both tangibly and intangibly?

Risk-taking problems:

- What major, specific barriers and obstacles might you encounter?
- Who will resist, impede, or subvert your risk the most?
- What, if anything, can you do to limit or prevent this?

Risk-taking solutions:

- Which problems can you avoid or prevent, and how will you do that?

- Which problems can you limit, contain, or reduce, and how will you do that?
- What can you do to survive problems you can't avoid, prevent, or limit?

Risk-taking resources:

- What people are key to implementing your plan?
- Which of their skills do you need?
- What do you need to do to enlist their support, even if you can require their participation?
- How much of their time do you need?
- What other resources do you need (such as materials, equipment, money, consultants, and training)?
- What budget do you need for your plan, including initial capital investment and any operating cost adjustments?

Risk-taking activities:

- What steps in what sequence will achieve your risk-taking goal(s)?
- How much time will each step require?
- What could sabotage the plans at any step?

LIMIT DANGER

The largest number of risk reduction tactics fall into the category of limiting danger. With so many elements in any management risk, and so few that can be controlled, it is important to concentrate on reducing the number of elements that pose threats. The most effective methods include bargaining for more time, obtaining better information, preventing dangerous escalation, managing experts more thoroughly, adjusting to the risk context, and adapting technology risk tactics. Risk dangers can always be reduced to some degree with skillful use of these tactics.

Negotiate Time Extensions

Even a few extra hours or days can be enough time to allow for danger-countering actions. Risk-taking deadlines, for example, can often be renegotiated, even if they have been firmly set. Schedulers will usually consider adjusting a time frame when convinced that the outcome will benefit all parties involved.

Time extensions increase your ability to control and offset potential hazards. More time expands the range of risk-limiting options you can identify and put in place. The actions may or may not work. But without the opportunity to take them, you may never know whether the risk could have been managed more safely.

Obtain Better Information

Better information provides you with a reliable road map for risk taking, allowing you to navigate around dead ends and through detours more efficiently. Better information also permits moving ahead more swiftly and taking advantage of narrow windows of opportunity.

The more you know about the uncertainties—what they are, what factors increase them, how often they occur, how to deal with them—the safer your risk venture. As discussed in Chapter Five, invest sufficient, but not excessive, time and money in research. Collecting too much information wastes resources; worse, it can lead to rash abandonment of the venture. Researching the "bad news" only reinforces the common practice of prejudging risks negatively.

Find and fill in the large gaps in your risk information, but don't try to plug every small hole. Search for useful and up-to-date information, not more quantities of it. And pay attention to the visibility of your research activities, as they could tip off your opponents.

One of the trade-offs of using information to reduce risks is that research can be surprisingly expensive. Advice attributed to former Harvard University president Derek Bok ("If you think education is expensive, try ignorance") can be adapted to help you justify your budget: if you think risk information is expensive, try paying for avoidable risk failures.

Adjust to the Risk Context

Modify your decisions and the mode of implementation to suit current conditions in your organizational unit. Is this the right time to take the risk? What will be the impact of the current organization mood? Do you have the financial reserves to pay for damages incurred? Peter Keen, chairman of the International Center for Information Technologies, recommends this tactic: "In my experience, the management risk context, such as what specific division or branch is impacted, determines the boundaries of permissible management risk taking. What equals high or low risk in one management context doesn't equal the same in another. The limits of risk failure in one management context don't match the limits in another as well. What may seem like an innovative risk in one management context may very well seem like a traditional one in another. You probably have a clear sense of whether your organization generally supports or criticizes risk taking. Part of adjusting the size of each risk is checking out whether the risk-taking environment has changed in ways endangering its success" (Keen, 1991).

Prevent Danger Escalation

Danger escalation occurs when you invest more resources into a venture than you had originally planned. Raising the risk ceiling raises the potential losses but not necessarily the potential gains.

To prevent escalation, set and stick to loss limits. Know, for example, when to stop spending unbudgeted resources to "buy off" dangers. For Rebecca Klemm, president of her own policy research and analysis firm, recognizing when to say no and yes to risk investment is a judgment call learned through experience. "You can and must cap your risk investment, putting limits on your time, energy, and money . . . but this is very difficult to do. It's hard to stop because so much is at stake, including your ego and reputation. Somehow, you have to have the strength to say, 'That's enough'" (1992).

The more audacious and uncertain your risk, the greater the need to set measurable loss limits at the start. In doing so, include the costs of implementing your danger prevention tactics. The goal is always to get the most risk security for the smallest expenditure of resources.

You can prevent excessive escalation of a risk project by asking yourself or others if these symptoms describe your management of it (adapted from Straw and Ross, 1987):

- Difficulty in defining or recognizing warning signs of impending project failure

- Tying personal and career success to the project's success

- Blaming the messenger for project-killing messages

- Continually bailing out the project at the expense of other projects or work

- Feeling that "if this project ends, I'll be devastated" or anything close to that

- Evaluating others' competence or loyalty on the basis of their support for the project

- Discounting repeated project dangers as merely "expected" or "temporary"

As these indicators of risk escalation imply, a fuzzy line separates productive persistence from unproductive stubbornness in managing risks. An unforeseeable deluge of setbacks to your risk, for example, could justify every one of these otherwise risk-escalating symptoms. Chances are good, however, that you can tell whether unique circumstances justify them by means of ruthless self-honesty.

But if this still leaves you unsure, ask yourself if one or more of the following conclusions apply: (1) you would cancel the risk project if you took over your own job for the first time today, (2) the opportunity-cost trade-offs fail to justify investing any more resources in the risk project, or (3) the coercive pressure to escalate the risk investment comes almost totally from yourself (Straw and Ross, 1987). If so, you have probably crossed the line between a fruitful, "will-do" risk management mentality and a sterile, "won't-do" one.

If you even suspect you have crossed the line from prudent to imprudent risk escalation, act quickly. Make a prompt decision about when and how to stop risk escalation and act on it. Doing so prevents a modest and affordable flop from turning into a large-scale, unafford-able disaster.

Manage Experts Effectively

Employing the knowledge, perspective, insights, and experience of experts can help you defuse dangers. But unless you manage them properly, you may end up with useless advice.

In hiring experts to reduce your risk, provide a written summary of what you need. Write down any concerns you have regarding their service. If you are concerned about the possibility of their hiding bad news, or failing to put jargon into understandable terms, put it in writing. Most experts will respond fully to your concerns and welcome joint efforts to clarify the goals of their services.

In screening and hiring experts, evaluate the limits of their expertise. Separate what they may know about the problem from that which nobody really knows for sure. Ask potential consultants, "How would you rate the current level of practical understanding of this subject on a scale of 1 to 10 among qualified experts? Assume 10 equals totally scientific, complete, understanding of this area, and 1 equals the opposite." Even if your consultants know the state-of-the-art in your area, there may still be huge gaps in their understanding, which may cause your danger-minimizing actions to backfire. "It is not enough to claim that 'these are the ranking experts in the field.' for there are some fields in which the most knowledgeable individuals understand a relatively small proportion of all there is to be known" (Fischhoff, Slovic, and Lichtenstein, 1981, p. 193). In other words, make your own appraisal of the credibility of the expert.

Require experts to stay within the limits of what they know. If you push them beyond their documented abilities, expect them to be fallible, as you are asking for speculation. In trying to please you, they may resort to speculative advice. "When forced to go beyond the limits of the available data or convert their incomplete knowledge into judgments usable by risk assessors (like you), they may fall back on the intuitive process, just like everyone else" (p. 190).

Experts, like managers, also suffer now and then from overconfidence in their knowledge and judgment. Such excessive confidence contributed, for example, to scientists' failure to spot the harmful effects of X-rays until use had become widespread and injurious to millions of people.

In work organizations committed to total quality, asking "why?" five times is accepted as a tool for preventing and eliminating any quality-related problems (Imai, 1986). The method can also serve to reduce the impact of flawed or incomplete information on your risk. When asking why, however, be sure to do so in a way that doesn't sound childishly repetitive. Explain to them, for instance, how this technique brings you both closer to finding the "root cause" of potential risk hazards and can lead to their prevention.

The inability of consultants to reach consensus can prove time-consuming and can complicate your risk reduction actions. Two guidelines may help with this problem (Fischhoff, Slovic, and Lichtenstein, 1981). First, accept the limits of informed speculation when it is the best experts can provide in the absence of systematic, reliable data. Second, use several experts and place your course of action somewhere in the middle of their range of recommendations. Seeking a second or third expert opinion can prevent many a risk-taking disaster. A third tactic is to always question intensively and aggressively each expert's assumptions, data, and research methods. Limits of evidence and understanding occur in every field of expertise.

In real life, experts can rarely provide the single right answer to your risk questions. Try to obtain the best available advice within the limits of your time and budget. Doing any less forfeits one of your best chances to limit danger.

Adapt Technology Risk Tactics

Any organization taking technology-intensive risks can profit from NASA's model of risk minimization. NASA's tactics can also be applied to a wide range of risks not necessarily related to technology (Broad, 1986).

Anticipate greater riskiness at the beginning of a venture. NASA estimates the risk of catastrophic failure during the blazing liftoff into orbit of any single space shuttle flight at one in seventy-eight. These are the odds of destroying the shuttle and killing the astronauts along with it. The launch carries the greatest risks of the entire flight.

The same applies to management risks in general. What are the "launch" dangers associated with your risk? How can they be detected or mitigated? What is the greatest danger when the organizational engines are "running at high speeds and high temperature"?

NASA has learned to remain skeptical about risk failure calculation. Managers should view their own calculations in the same light. How might you verify risk danger estimates? In what ways could your doubts or hopes bias calculations? Has anything changed to justify recalculating the risk? Has the risk environment changed in ways that reduce the validity of the calculations? The Challenger failure occurred because the spacecraft was operating in colder weather than design calculations had anticipated.

Guard against complacency as you grow more successful in your risking. NASA's many impressive successes lulled managers into underestimating potential hazards. Prior to the Challenger, NASA "officials regularly asserted that the chance of disaster was 1 flight in 100,000." This conflicted with an Air Force prediction "that of the 14 major accidents that might destroy the shuttle, booster failure was the most likely, with chances of 1 flight in 35." As a manager, guard against downplaying potential danger, no matter how successful your risk-taking record. Spend less time arguing about the odds of danger and more time reducing them.

The longer you succeed in risk taking, the more vigilant you must be. There is a good chance failure will strike eventually. The Challenger tragedy overshadowed NASA's impressive string of successes up to that time: twenty-four shuttle flights and forty-three Delta launches.

Watch the details of your venture. They can undo your plans just as effectively as larger factors can. As one NASA specialist put it, "We lost [the Challenger shuttle] for a stupid reason, because the simplest part of the system failed." Avoid actions that will increase your vulnerability to problems related to the smaller, seemingly simple aspects of the risk. Since 1971, NASA had "cut by 71 percent the number of people responsible for monitoring the quality and reliability of its equipment." Reducing investment in quality control increases exposure to failure of "the simplest part of the system."

At the same time, track the most critical dangers obsessively. NASA uses the term "Critical One" for factors that, by themselves, could cause a mission failure. They listed 748 Critical One items on the space shuttle and orbiter at the time of the Challenger explosion.

What are the critical factors in your risk? Search for them relentlessly. Try to anticipate events most likely to set the Critical One factors in motion, and determine the possible consequences. Then weigh the feasibility of a Plan B.

However successfully or unsuccessfully a risk turns out, recall your experience with each Critical One factor. NASA analyzes and revises its Critical One list after each shuttle mission. The more you know and can control the Critical One elements of your risk, the safer you'll be.

Decide how safe is safe. The more complex the risk, the greater the chances for things to go wrong. The goal is to reduce danger to an acceptable level. The following principles, developed by NASA, may help you decide how safe is safe for your own risks. While they were developed for technology-related ventures, they can be effectively applied to other types of risks.

- *Prototype Design:* Explore all foreseeable hazards based on experience with similar ventures. Incorporate the findings into an imaginary walk-through or, if applicable, conceptual or physical prototype.

- *Fail-Safe Systems:* Even if you have none, imagine what a fail-safe system would be like for the risk. This may reveal overlooked dangers, or suggest actions that could reduce your exposure to them.

- *Reliability Testing:* With another manager, or with a team of devil's advocates, test the risk plan for weaknesses. Ask your colleagues to critique it.

- *Field Experience:* Compare the expected performance with the actual performance of the risk. Probe for all lessons to be learned, especially those you can do something about in future ventures.

- *Routine Inspections:* Monitor the quality of all work going into the risk. Far better, design all procedures to build in the highest levels of quality.

- *Safety Limits:* Keep the risk within the known limits of safety.

SHARE THE DANGER

In addition to "spreading risk around," the easily abused tactic unveiled in Chapter Three, there are a number of ways to reduce danger by sharing it with others, including the creation of alliances, consortia, partnerships, or joint ventures. Pooling intellectual and financial resources limits the amount of loss experienced by any one party and increases the willingness to pursue hazardous ventures.

Groups, generally speaking, are more likely than individuals to take bigger risks.

Negotiate risk-sharing arrangements fairly, openly, and in writing. Aim for agreements on risk information gathering, danger reduction tactics, and shared-cost estimates.

Bear in mind the factors that can weaken the effectiveness of a risk-sharing alliance:

- Greater complexity, making the implementation process more cumbersome
- Greater amounts of time and effort needed to reach consensus
- Quibbling over credits
- Smaller gains for each participant in exchange for reduced risk
- More opportunities for mistakes due to miscommunication and poor coordination
- The possibility of incompetence, negligence, or dishonesty
- Disagreements that can slow responsiveness and threaten internal unity

A perfectly legitimate way to share danger is to build consensus for the risk. An open and informative approach to risk sharing gives key participants the option of becoming limited or unlimited partners, so to speak, in the venture. Richard Lesher, president of the U.S. Chamber of Commerce, builds consensus on the need to risk at an early stage: "I try to generate as much consensus for the risk as I can. I ask staff and volunteer leaders in the Chamber, for example, to help me pinpoint, rank, and limit the key uncertainties of the risk, especially those impacting the Chamber and its members in any pivotal ways. Some level of consensus is extra important from those members whose support is critical to the success of the risk venture. I usually bring them all together, encourage candid debate, and listen carefully to the pros and cons they raise. This builds risk-taking commitment and ownership. And I always involve our Board of Directors, my first-level risk-sharing partners, early on" (1992).

Peter Keen, chairman of the International Center for Information Technologies, offers another tactic for sharing the hazards of risk taking: creating a prospectus modeled after brochures issued by investment firms (1991). Generally speaking, a prospectus describes "the major features of a proposed business venture in enough detail so that prospective investors, participants, or buyers may evaluate it" (*Random House Dictionary*). A management risk prospectus should present the pros and cons of the proposed venture factually and clearly, just as an investment prospectus would. Keen warns against understating either the pros or cons in the risk "investment prospectus, as this could cause you serious trouble later, such as losing your credibility or tainting your reputation." Using a prospectus could secure a favorable review of your proposed venture at the outset, as well as some amount of protection from recrimination later if it fails.

REDUCING MANAGEMENT RISKS AT MCI

The organizational environment of MCI Communications is aggressively risk-oriented. Senior vice president Carol Herod has learned to adapt her decision making to fit MCI's unique corporate culture. Her methods of reducing the dangers of risk taking employ a number of the tactics presented in this chapter.

Most of the people who work at MCI are risk takers, even if they never think of themselves that way. After all, we're still pretty much a David fighting Goliath, and anyone who chooses to work here knows that. People who can't take this risk-taking environment tend to leave quickly.

Risk taking is an accepted mode of behavior here at MCI, no matter what you do. When you take a risk here that does not work, a sincere apology is usually enough. You're expected to admit and communicate your mistakes and to promise to apply these lessons the next time.

Of course we often make wrong decisions, and we do hear about it. But we never get beaten up by higher management for our goofs. You can get addicted easily to that kind of decision-making freedom and trust.

At MCI, not taking risks will get you in more trouble than taking them. There's no room for complacency or staying "close to the wall" around here. We thrive on change, and that means almost everyone in this company takes risks. But you can bet everyone is very careful and prudent about how and when they take any risk.

I learned a lot about limiting the downside of my risk with a new marketing program we created and introduced a few years ago. My first reaction to the idea was that it was a high-risk move. I was totally wrong in guessing the major risks of the new service.

As it turned out, our greatest risks were technology related. Figuring out how the service would show up on customer bills was extremely complicated. We didn't know how we were going to do it and we had to move very fast. Our first technical design solution, for instance, identified only about half the problems we would encounter.

We reduced this huge corporate-level risk several ways. First, we developed an advertising strategy positioning the new service positively, using well-known actors giving this new idea credibility. Second, we used "teaser" advertisements describing the service in general terms, giving us time to work out the details, as well as to stop the competition from stealing our idea. Third, we introduced the service to selected segments within our current customer base—people unlikely to be offended by this unconventional kind of service. Fourth, we tested and refined several improvements in our direct mail strategy and technology.

One way I reduce any major risk is by creating extra communication lines and channels. Without generating much extra work, using electronic mail, I make sure everyone stays informed on any important developments in the risk activity. Part of this is making it acceptable to reveal problems or express concerns without worrying about blame or embarrassment. Sometimes, for example, I have daily conference calls so we can surface and resolve problems sooner and quicker. While it takes time to do it, constant communication among your risk team enables you to stay in greater control of your risk and limit its surprises [Herod, 1992].

8

SURVIVE THE FAILURES: DEALING WITH THE DOWNSIDE OF RISK

There is encouraging news about the consequences of risk failure. They are survivable. You are far from helpless in the face of punishment. Once you know how to alleviate some of the more painful aftereffects of an unsuccessful risk, you need not fear the aftermath as an unbearable ordeal. It is even possible to gain long-term payoffs from the experience.

The approaches to limiting the penalties of initiating a risk are numerous and varied. They include assembling safety nets of supporters and professional contacts; profiting from your venture by failing selectively and failing early; communicating honestly and openly about the risk-taking process; converting failure to learning by extracting lessons from your mistakes; shielding your self-respect by being resilient and focusing on growth; and risking responsibly by pursuing reasonable, realistic, and calculated courses of action.

There is no ignoring the fact that the consequences of risk failure can be costly. For some people, they include an increased tendency to avoid risking in the future. Allowing the fear of failure to have that effect would be a mistake. After all, losses can occur even if you choose the seemingly safe option of not risking.

A word of advice to those tempted to dismiss psychological survival tactics: doing so can deprive you of the opportunity to gain support when you need it most. Without such guidelines, you may have much more difficulty coping with the consequences of failed actions, both in the present and in the future. Applying effective tactics, on the other hand, may help you to turn the experience into a positive one, allowing you to claim and receive the credit due for responsible management risk taking. That is the least any manager can expect in surviving a risk failure.

ASSEMBLE SAFETY NETS

Responsible managers walk the risk tightrope only after placing a number of strong, durable safety nets underneath and inspecting them frequently.

These safety nets are made up of trusted colleagues, personal survival mechanisms, risk-taking justifications and rationales, and professional resources.

You reinforce the effectiveness of risk safety nets by increasing their quality and quantity. When assembling a net of people, for example, find the ones you can count on to help you survive—people who will stick by you in spirit and in deed when the risk fails. Expand the net by increasing the number of people supporting the risk unequivocally.

Assemble a personal risk survival net by getting your personal finances in order, taking care of any major interpersonal or psychological problems, and asking relatives to support you in surviving the risk failure.

Assemble a net of rationales by clarifying the risk-taking justifications. Be able to defend your management decisions. Strengthen this net by asking yourself if the rationale is consistent with the organization's values and critical needs.

Strengthen the net of professional resources by adding new people to your network, pre-negotiating termination parachutes, building stronger ties with your weaker contacts, and reinforcing relationships with your closest contacts. In addition, continue to develop marketable skills.

Masters at risk taking maintain and check their safety nets routinely, not just before venturing a risk. Letting the safety net deteriorate puts you in jeopardy when walking the risk tightrope. The last minute is not the best time to contemplate repairs.

SQUEEZE SMALL PROFITS FROM LARGE LOSSES

The more costly your risk failure, the better the opportunity to extract some offsetting compensation from it. To recoup a portion of your investment, you need not be the world's shrewdest negotiator. You do need average amounts of qualities and skills you now possess or can surely generate for this purpose: vision, audacity, discretion, planning, ambition, and perseverance. And you only need two of these at a time.

You reduce in advance the net cost of a risk-taking calamity by intentionally taking risks so that if you fail, you do it *grandly* (with vision and audacity), *judiciously* (with discretion and planning), or *immediately* (with ambition and perseverance).

Fail on a Large Scale

Risk survival tactics rest on two laws. Law Number One states that the bigger the risk, the greater the tendency to blame failure on the risk. Law Number Two asserts the opposite: the smaller the risk, the greater the tendency to blame failure on the risk taker.

In a twist of logic, failing on a monumental scale sometimes pays off quite well. Managers experiencing large-scale failures often receive forgiveness more readily than if their risks had been small. Other managers may respond with expressions of admiration rather than negative criticism. Those who think and act boldly command a certain respect for their foresight and drive, regardless of the outcome.

How do they get away with it? First, by the risks they select—risks that address urgent crises, achieve major breakthroughs, or eliminate migraine-size organizational headaches. Second, they conduct the risk in exemplary fashion, as by researching every aspect as completely as possible. Third, they generate abundant support at all levels to defend its failure. Fourth, they sometimes benefit from the sheer chutzpah of tilting at big windmills.

Fail Selectively

Managers seem entitled to a few failures now and then. Normally, the more risks you take successfully, the larger the number and size of risks you are permitted to take unsuccessfully. Failing selectively means picking your risks with discrimination, which means knowing, for example, whether your career and your department can afford a failure. It also means getting to know what kind of risk failure your organization will tolerate.

The decision to use any of your hard-to-come-by risk failure chits requires careful planning. Ask yourself such questions as "Should I risk anything in this endeavor?" "Can I afford a failure at this time and in this way?" No one expects you to succeed with every risk; just be sure to succeed enough to protect your option to risk again in the future.

Fail Early

Al Neuharth, founder of *USA Today,* advocates taking big risks earlier rather than later in your career. The more you do so, the more skill and knowledge you will have for taking and recovering from later risks. Even if your early, big ventures fail, they often spur you to subsequent success. The bigger the failure, the greater the long-term, compensating benefits. Neuharth recommends failing in a big way before reaching age forty. "You will fail when you're old enough to really learn something from it, but still young enough to start over" (1989, p. 8).

Neuharth's own failure at age twenty-nine left him and a close friend bankrupt and heavily in debt. They lost fifty thousand dollars raised from small stockholders on a sports newspaper printed on peach-colored paper. To this day, Neuharth believes his fanatical determination to overcome that early failure led to later success on a grand scale. His "learn early from risk failure" tactic works best, of course, for those responding in a similar way to their own disasters. As always, knowing yourself is integral to "successful" failure. At a minimum, however, Neuharth's view underscores the importance of fighting back and focusing on what can be learned from risk failure, regardless of the magnitude.

There are two ways to make the most of this tactic. First, analyze your early failure exhaustively. Squeeze from it every relevant and useful lesson you can find, like an archeologist hunting for fragile treasure. Search systematically. Dig deeply. Sift slowly. And verify each discovery for its authenticity.

Second, accept full responsibility for the early failure. Resist the temptation to blame others. Resist blaming yourself—there is no failure, only feedback.

The following true story sheds further light on the long-term value of early failures. It comes from Ted Wiss (1993), an executive with over twenty years of experience in marketing high technology to Fortune 1,000 firms.

A major risk I took early in my career was embarking on a new business venture in a high technology firm. I invested heavily in the venture. I literally bet my house and life savings on the deal—and lost. It failed for many reasons, such as misreading the market for our product, undercapitalization, and internal politics.

I had to start all over, financially, personally, and professionally. Worst of all, it was tough for my family for quite a while. We had to lower our standard of living. These losses seemed like a lot back then, but not any more. In the long run, I've been able to more than make it all up to them. I have to admit though, I wish I could have learned these risk-taking lessons in less costly ways.

I learned, the hard way, risk-taking lessons I've cashed in on over the years. Lessons like how to legally protect myself and the organization better, how to hold top management's feet closer to the fire, and how to select risk partners who can take the pressures of high-level risk taking and not compromise themselves ethically at the same time. Few people understand that failure happens to persistent risk takers, yet that's what we have to do in the marketing field, no matter how much we try to reduce the unknown factors of risking.

When your risk starts getting you down, remind yourself of three things. First, worries and frustrations are a kind of necessary evil that seem to tag along with risk taking, regardless of how the risk turns out. Second, a few years from whatever happens, the source of your worries and frustrations probably won't matter very much. Third, even if the worst outcome happens, odds are you'll figure out a way to handle it. And fourth, things will go wrong regardless of how much you worry—so why worry?

Wiss profited from his lesson by continuing to risk. He bet that another start-up technology firm he joined had a great future. The firm was picked in 1991 as a top stock to watch by both *USA Today* and the *Wall Street Journal.* As vice president for sales and marketing, Wiss doubled sales two years in a row. He saw his own stock in the firm more than double as well, but, because of internal management problems, the firm's stock plummeted. Wiss took another big risk by leaving the firm in an attempt to pressure the board of directors to make drastic changes in the firm's management, which it did— eventually. His stock in the firm later rebounded more than sixfold. Wiss may be an exceptionally risk-oriented executive, but his experiences show that it is possible to profit from risk in spite of failure.

MITIGATE PENALTIES

The risk penalty process can be mortifying. Its effects on your career and business can last a long time. Never delude yourself about this potential when you do battle in the risk arena. Yet the penalties for taking elective management risks, for example, are probably as wildly exaggerated as the career payoffs for taking mandated ones.

There are ways to lessen the duration and severity of the punishment experience. Balk at becoming too submissive or too willing a risk casualty. Initiate action to mitigate the penalty process. The following Eight A's of communicating failure can improve your effectiveness in blunting risk penalties:

- **A**dmit the failure without excusing or defending yourself or your team.

- **A**nnounce the failure first and privately to the person to whom you report.

- **A**pologize for the negative consequences of the failure.

- **A**im any humor at yourself alone.

- **A**ct as calm and composed, but not unconcerned, as your nature allows.

- **A**nswer questions about the failure honestly and fully.

- **A**ccept any expressions of condolence with grace and gratitude.

- **A**cknowledge the outstanding work of your risk associates publicly and sincerely.

Rebecca Klemm, president of Klemm Analysis Group, Inc., keeps the communication lines open throughout the risk-taking process, which helps to moderate any negative consequences.

> I've learned over the years to quickly and openly admit my weak points. In the case of risk taking, I point out risk-taking deficiencies beforehand and announce our risk-taking mistakes afterwards.
> Just as a successful sales manager anticipates the buyer's concerns and objections, I take the lead in presenting a risk-taking weakness or error. That way I control how negative aspects of risk qualifications or risk performance are perceived. This also allows me the chance to at least try to turn something negative into something positive [Klemm, 1992].

File a Risk Insurance Claim

As a manager, you automatically receive a kind of risk "insurance policy." Similar to a safety net, this hypothetical insurance protects you, to some degree, against failure and its penalties. Like real insurance, the policy has deductibles (the amount of penalty you must pay) and premiums.

The minimum eligibility requirements, the scope of

coverage, and the deductibles differ for each profession and organization. Certain qualifications increase your individual coverage. They include your integrity, competence, commitment, and creativity.

The standard policy provides one primary benefit: the right to one mistake. Not just any mistake, but a special kind—one that is inventive, accidental, and honest. These kinds of mistakes usually prove cost-effective, if only in the long term. Think of Ford's mistake with the Edsel discussed earlier. Ford ultimately gained by applying the expensive lesson to the production of the profitable Mustang series.

There is a second risk insurance benefit: the right to blame. Used primarily by unprincipled managers, this benefit permits the "policy holder" to blame the failure on forces beyond human control: the competition, scheduling problems, miscommunication, uncooperative units, incompetent work associates, the subcontractors, the weather, and so on. Each of these factors could be legitimate explanations for risk failure, but not when used dishonestly. They are a refuge for incompetent and unethical risk takers.

CONVERT FAILURE
TO LEARNING

Learning from mistakes facilitates future success. As the late Dr. Laurence J. Peter, author of *The Peter Principle,* observed, "There are two kinds of failures, those who thought and never did, and those who did and never thought" (1979, p. 177). This is another way of saying failure hurts us only when we ignore its gifts: awareness, information, and insight. The only failure is failing to learn from the lessons of unexpected outcomes.

Charlotte Taylor, president of a management consulting firm, attests to the impact on learning of doing things wrong. "Risk failures and missed opportunities cause you to change your thinking. They give you a needed whack on the head. Sometimes, this is the only way one will ever focus totally to learn from mistakes.

"If you're willing to look for them, every risk failure teaches important lessons. When your risk fails, you have to dig for the lessons in it, and keep on risking. Sometimes they're hard to find. It may take months or years to discover them" (Taylor, 1992).

Find a manager with excellent judgment and you will meet one who made many mistakes.

Master risk takers go so far as to dispute the very notion of failure and question the standard criteria for judging success. Laura Henderson, president of a large consulting firm, admits, "I probably measure success differently than most managers. I don't measure it just in terms of quarterly profits, but in terms of what I learn and how it impacts the organization. My criterion of success is whether it's going to be easier to do more business because we made a decision. You have to be careful about stamping tough management decisions as 'successes' or 'failures'" (1992).

MCI executive Carol Herod believes that failure, if handled with common sense and creativity, can be salvaged and turned into success, even if that means, in her words, ending up at Point K instead of at Point X:

> I have trouble seeing any risk as a "failure" because that word sounds so absolute and final to me. To me, risk taking means facing many decision points and redefining the risk every time you reach one. Of course, if my risk-taking destination is Point X, I often end up at Point K instead. But when I do, I can nearly always adapt to Point K in some positive way. I don't see a risk as a "failure" just because I

never get to my original Point X risk-taking
destination.

For example, I left my telecommunications
firm for another company, my Point X in this case.
I ended up instead at a Point K, back to the original
company. I had discovered I didn't fit into the other
company's management culture. I view ending up
where I didn't expect to be a risk-taking success, not
a failure. [Carol was recently promoted to one of the
highest senior management positions in her
company.]

To make this tactic work for you, always make
sure you start communicating up and down the organization as soon as you know you're headed toward Point K instead of Point X. In addition,
conduct an in-depth "post-mortem" with your team,
identifying all the lessons learned and sharing them
with others. When you end up at Point K, you need
to work extra hard at helping your team and super-
visor appreciate the positive gains of your risk venture, even if Point K seems like a lousy place to end
up (Herod, 1992).

Making the most of these situations requires the difficult response of accepting the unchosen rewards as
gratefully as we would the ones we hoped to receive. And
it involves another difficult process: allowing the ego to
convert failures into learning. It may help to note Dr. Peter's other observation about the challenge of learning
from mistakes: "Success goes to your head, failure to your
heart" (1979, p. 177). The emotional pain of failure may
block the ability to learn from the experience.

Gaining from mistakes also requires looking for all
the relevant lessons in your failure. Lessons like these:
why your brilliant idea was fatally flawed; specific
ways the execution of your tactics, not the tactics themselves, contributed to the failure; the greater than assumed limits to controlling what sabotaged your risk; or

innovative ways to recover even larger amounts of your sunk costs, as William R. T. Oakes, president of a management firm, has learned: "You learn the most from both your risk-taking successes and failures much later on, not right after they've happened. What you think is a big failure at the moment can turn out to be the foundation for an even bigger success later. And vice versa. There have been several times when an initial business success lost money later and an initial business failure made money eventually. Management risk taking, I believe, demands 'stepping out of expectations' now and then, both your own and others" (Oakes, 1991).

No management risk ever fails completely. Managers interviewed confirm a silver lining inside the cloud of each risk outcome, commonly labeled "lessons learned." It may take a long time for these compensatory lessons to emerge, but they always do. By being attentive, you are sure to discover the long-term success in every seeming failure.

Joyce Doria, vice president of an international technology and management consulting firm, told the following story of a risk she took that failed, and what happened to her as a result.

> One of the biggest management risks I took was while trying to penetrate the aerospace systems training market, a new market for the firm at the time. I lacked convincing proof of our ability to perform in this market, as well as the investment cash to support this new market.
>
> The potential gains included expanding corporate capability, increasing profits, and broadening my practice area; in other words, giving it greater stability and diversity. Most importantly, it would give me a solid platform for making partner—THE big goal of mine from the day I joined the firm.
>
> If my risk failed, my credibility as a partner-track candidate would be damaged severely, along

with my practice area's reputation. Then there would be the "opportunity cost" of all that non-billable work time, plus a loss of personal time invested. Before we could get a foothold in this market, our potential clients ran into bad business times, much like those suffering from the recession today. Our competitors, with strong track records and client bases, locked up what little business there was.

Surprisingly, this failure helped me and my group a lot and hurt us very little. Because of the way we took this risk, everyone believed it was the risk that failed, not us, and that the risk was a smart one and the undermining economic circumstances were beyond anyone's control.

But don't assume I got off unscathed. Some colleagues criticized me for not making more realistic projections about the cost, timing, and barriers of the new market. My ego was bruised, more than I ever admitted to anyone. My personal life suffered from all the time, worry, and travel the risk demanded. And I lost a fair amount of income by having to wait another full year to make partner.

Many indispensable lessons resulted from my risk-taking failure in penetrating a new market during my first years at the firm. I learned:

- To select my risk-taking team more carefully, checking, for example, their resilience and flexibility under stress

- To fight harder for corporate resources without being concerned about appearing too aggressive

- To play more hardball, fighting longer to keep from getting shoved into dead ends by competitors as well as by people in my own organization

- To be unafraid of being branded what today would be called an "Iron Lady"

- To charge after my top goals resolutely, no matter how strong the opposition and criticism

- To forgive myself later for what I couldn't realistically have expected to have known or anticipated before taking a risk, and

- To appreciate the lessons I learn from risk taking, even if the outcome wasn't what I hoped it would be.

No management risk decision is as final or as "make it or break it" as you fear. You can survive most any risk-taking problem. And you can always create another risk-taking opportunity. You think "the world will end" if a risk decision backfires, but of course, it's still there when you wake up [Doria, 1992].

SHIELD SELF-RESPECT

When a risk fails, you have a choice. You can focus on self-improvement or on self-punishment. Risk experts agree that you should reject the self-punishment option and embrace the growth alternative.

Even the best manager makes erroneous judgments occasionally. Yet many managers cling to an unrealistic and almost arrogant expectation of infallibility. This increases the potential for damage to self-esteem when a failure does occur. Shield your self-respect by refusing to condemn yourself for your lack of perfect foresight. Rid yourself of the notion that you can foretell the future with precision. Risk experts label this phenomenon *presentism,* or the natural tendency to overstate what could have been foreseen in advance of any risk venture, to believe one should have anticipated events much better than was actually possible. Presentism also causes you to lower your ego shield against failure when you exaggerate in hindsight what you knew in foresight (Fisch-hoff, Slovic, and Lichtenstein, 1981). In other words, you delude yourself into believing you knew more about a risk before taking it than you actually knew or could have known.

Buffer your self-esteem by being resilient in the face of anger, embarrassment, and loss. How? By "cleaning up" as quickly as possible; by applying the lessons learned; by refusing to punish yourself for errors of omission and commission; by respecting your own honest intentions and best efforts; and by believing resolutely you will end up better off some day for having taken the risk.

No matter how disastrous the outcome of your risk endeavor, avoid any feeling of regret. When you take risks, even when they fail, your self-esteem usually increases. You feel legitimately proud for displaying the courage of your convictions. You know you stretched and pushed yourself beyond self-set boundaries. And your friends will probably express their respect for your tenacity, which will help you survive the psychological hardships of failure.

RISK RESPONSIBLY

You survive failure more easily if you take the risk responsibly. Responsible risks are calculated, reasonable, and realistic. They advance the interests of the manager and the organization without placing either in jeopardy. By taking a risk responsibly, you increase the odds of a "lightened sentence" or bearable censure if it fails.

Responsible risk taking is distinguished by the amount of accountability assumed; by the initiative, determination, and flexibility of the risk taker; by the quality of the analysis, research, and planning; by the caution and moderation applied to estimates of payoffs

and penalties; and by the informed support of all participants. Risking responsibly means achieving a delicate
balance between daring and caution.

Arthur I. Hersh, president and CEO of a computer
software consortium, asserts that responsible risk takers "think long and hard about the consequences of their
risk taking on all parties involved, from the unit to the
shareholders to the customers. And they do the best they
can to balance the different interests of all parties affected by the outcome of the risk. In addition, responsible risk takers shoulder a fair share of the criticism and
costs if the risk fails" (1992).

In the view of business school professor Richard
Donnelly (1991), "'responsible' management risk taking
exhibits a number of qualities: exemplary personal and
professional integrity; a justifiable strategic-level objective; and an extensive, but reasonable, review of existing
data. Take a stand personally and tell the next management level what you truly believe, not what will appease
them, and be totally aboveboard about the positive and
negative sides to the risk."

Risking responsibly means attempting to outma-
neuver any threat to the risk's success. "When a risk
falters, risk takers move to fix it, not place the blame.
When something fails they immediately analyze why
and start scouting the next step" (Kehrer, 1989, p. 85).
This kind of vigilance helps you to survive if the risk
flounders in the end.

Taking risks responsibly demands that you accept
deserved blame, from honest mistakes, and repair the
damage as much as possible. Some managers evade
these tasks by portraying themselves as tragic heroes, or
as well-meaning risk takers victimized by bad luck.
Those who risk responsibly behave differently. They admit their mistakes, without complaints or excuses, and
they clean up the wreckage of risk failure. In other
words, they pay the bills, file any reports, reassign per-

sonnel, return unused parts and supplies, and, if appropriate, close down the facility. Tie up all loose ends quickly and quietly. It is bad form to leave important tasks unresolved.

A responsibly undertaken risk deflects overly harsh and automatic criticism. But the advantages go beyond reducing penalties. Higher standards broaden managers' risk-taking discretion, while improving their efforts. Responsible risk taking is more than doing the right thing. It is doing things right.

PART THREE

Keeping Risk Alive: Encouraging Effective Risk Taking in Yourself and Others

9

NURTURE YOUR SKILLS:
LEARNING BY TAKING ACTION

A number of self-development tactics will enhance the risk skills you already possess, while extending the range of your knowledge and abilities. The tactics include gradually increasing the size of your risks, toughening your self-discipline, crediting your past experience, borrowing methods from other fields of activity, and allowing yourself to proceed with cautious optimism in spite of uncertainty. The goal is to cultivate your risk taking through conscious and ongoing effort.

ENLARGE RISKS
INCREMENTALLY

You can develop your abilities by prodding yourself to take measurably larger risks at a constant, if slow, rate of increase. Limiting yourself to the size of your current risk will stunt the development of your risk-taking skills. In addition, taking bigger risks increases the potential for greater gains. Few managers achieve their loftiest ambitions without a few risks that may have been larger than they preferred.

Like a pole-vaulting athlete in training, build up your endurance and skill incrementally, setting the risk bar slightly higher for each jump. Doing so provides you with a window of opportunity to build self-confidence as you piece together increasingly complex risk strategies.

ADAPT
MOUNTAINEERING TACTICS

With a little imagination, you can adapt mountain-climbing tactics to the practice of climbing management mountains. As in pole-vaulting, the growth in competence that comes from climbing ever-higher mountains parallels the progress that results from taking increasingly formidable management risks. The mountaineering analogy can be developed further.

Enjoy the Secondary Wins

Mountain climbers who succeed and survive learn to cherish their secondary wins: exercising and displaying the sheer artistry their risks demand; sharpening old skills and discovering new ones; experiencing the excitement of the activity; solving difficult problems; and toughening their convictions by testing them in action.

Like a mountaineer, broaden your enjoyment of risking beyond the thrill of winning the pursued trophy. "The great truth that climbing teaches us is that the physical struggle and the contemplative aim are parts of one indivisible whole" (Irving, [1938] 1984, p. 127). Mountaineers value the reflective, mental stimulation of climbing, regardless of whether they reach the summit. In similar fashion, prize the secondary wins of risk taking, such as the problems solved or the camaraderie created. A number of skill-enhancing payoffs are possible apart from the originally targeted goal.

Maintain Concentration

Rivet your attention on each action, study the environment intently, and scan the horizon continuously, looking as far ahead as your line of vision permits, just as mountaineers do. "Rock-climbers in particular, must face inward, their eyes fixed intently on details immediately before them; every tiny fissure and minute flake of stone can be crucial, a matter of life and death. Climbers must be intimate with their environment" (Loomis, 1987, p. 5). In the same way, scan and probe the risk environment, searching for any sign of danger.

Consider also the importance climbers place on their descent. Seasoned climbers know a victorious ascent can turn to tragedy on the way down—if, that is, they become careless for one second in carrying out seemingly simple actions. Like veteran mountain climbers, guard against complacency at any point during your risk journey, even after its apparent conclusion. You may have won the competitive bid, for example, but failed to complete the legal paperwork in time to prevent a successful counterbid.

Stay in Control

Use every precaution against calamities, but never trust them completely. Count instead on the prudent execution of each risk step. "[Climbers] have not placed great faith in the rope. The risk of falling has been controlled chiefly by adopting a particular stance on the slope, always keeping three points of contact with it, and proceeding in a slow and deliberate manner. The climber pauses at some resting point, studies the terrain, plans the next moves, perhaps moves forward just enough to test them, rests again, and then executes the moves to the next rest" (Loughman, 1984, pp. 146–147).

Solve the Problems

Break problems into smaller components until you isolate a part you can solve; then find another, continuing until the entire problem is resolved. This is one way climbers find solutions when they seem to be at a dead end: "there were no large holds—just little wrinkles called edges, many no wider than the thin side of a nickel. The challenge wasn't merely physical. It is also mental—like a mathematics problem almost. You start at the end and work backwards. Okay, you say to yourself, to get to that hold, I have to get to the hold before it with my right hand, which means my left foot will have to be on that little edge, which I can only do if I switch my feet in route" (Collins, 1990, p. 42).

Ask for help when you need it. Mountaineers trust a fellow climber who can voice even the slightest doubt—who is never "too proud to ask for help, too self-confident or too ignorant to see the need for special care" (Irving, [1938] 1984).

Practice Leadership

The leadership principles of mountain climbing and management risking have much in common. Mountain-climbing leaders, for instance, always distinguish between actions that endanger themselves and those that place others in jeopardy.

"A leader or a last man in the Alps absolutely must not fall. We may accept the fact that daring leaders will take risks, and that accidents can happen, provided every leader is aware of the distinction between the risks which no man may allow himself to take for his party even with their consent, and the risks which he may take for himself alone, but which his friends will be ill advised if they allow him to incur . . . a leader . . . before he takes a chance, must make certain that the risk will be confined to himself, supposing such certainty can ever be attained. When he has made as certain of this as he can, he must not fall" (Young, 1984, pp. 331–332).

In this same manner, managers must always determine in advance the dangers to others of their risk-taking strategies and actions. Just as mountain-climbing leaders must never forget the potentially deadly cost of their misjudgments and missteps, so must management leaders. This responsibility is indeed a heavy and solemn one, both psychologically and ethically.

Cross the Barriers

The ultimate barriers to risk taking result less from their material dangers, such as career ruin, than from their psychological dangers, such as fear of failure. "The barrier is an invisible obstacle—the point where your arms and your nerve will buckle and fail—the divide where impossibility begins, where everything is too much, the steepness, the sheerness, the not-yet known—a kind of break in the world, a space-warp, where the laws favoring your survival will stop applying and pure gravity take over" (Craig, 1987, p. 5).

PERMIT
CAUTIOUS OPTIMISM

Optimism—particularly well-founded optimism—facilitates and expedites the development of risk-taking skills. It cannot be hollow or counterfeit. It has to be cautious optimism—a reality-based predisposition to expect favorable outcomes and to act pragmatically and creatively to ensure them.

Cautious optimism helps you become a better risk taker in several ways: it spurs creativity in handling unexpected problems; it counteracts irrational, negative fantasies about the risk; it inspires dogged persistence in outlasting setbacks; and it promotes learning by inspiring real-world actions—the first-hand experiences from which one learns most quickly and unforgettably.

TAKE
UNACCEPTABLE RISKS

Unacceptable risks work much better than acceptable ones in toughening your self-discipline and developing your skill. Furthermore, restricting yourself to easily taken chances limits you to small gains. Losses from unacceptable risks accelerate mastery faster than gains from acceptable ones. Going hungry can strengthen more than gorging on scraps.

Fear, of course, is the factor determining how unacceptable a risk appears in the eyes of the risk taker. To get a more objective fix on what unacceptable risks you should upgrade to, answer this question: What is the maximum percentage of your annual budget you would spend in pursuing a risk greater than the biggest you have taken so far?

David Campbell, a psychologist at the Center for Creative Leadership, recommends another way of identifying your limit. Ask yourself how much, without causing personal disaster, you could afford to lose if you invested in something new and innovative. Then compare that dollar amount with the total financial value of your personal assets. The amounts most of us are willing to lose, even if quadrupled, probably add up to a small percentage of assets. Campbell believes such affordable risks generate little fun for the risk taker and limited benefits for the organization (1983).

Limiting yourself to acceptable risks demonstrates managerial common sense, however, in certain circumstances: when high gains are not needed; when you face a precarious situation in which the normally acceptable becomes unacceptable; when new senior executives change the definition of an unacceptable risk; and when acceptable risks are enough to advance your individual or organizational interests.

CHALLENGE
RISK NAYSAYERS

"The people I want to hear about are the people who take risks," said poet Robert Frost. Many managers, however, would prefer not to hear about them. Risking means challenging and changing the status quo, which puts the risk taker in the minority. Presenting a proposal often involves running a gauntlet of risk-opposed naysayers— usually well-meaning it-won't-work, this-is-not-the-time status quo defenders.

Your situation may not be so bleak. But if it is, brace yourself for attempts to reject your proposal. Anticipating their opposition gives you a small advantage. But no one pretends that fighting the antagonistic majority will be simple or uncomplicated. It requires all the political savvy you can muster.

VISUALIZE RISKS
IMAGINATIVELY

Previewing risks in your imagination provides two benefits, one motivational, the other pragmatic. First, doing so allows you to envision the positive aspects of the venture, which helps to inspire action. Second, it safeguards risking by permitting an exploration of the negative side.

Rehearsing your risk becomes a learning experience. You picture the real-life details, feelings, and experiences, and thus expand your understanding of them. You have the freedom to uncover hidden possibilities, both good and bad.

Psychologist Ellen Siegelman (1983) designed the following visualization exercise to facilitate the exploration of any risk. It is particularly helpful when you are just beginning to contemplate one. Find a quiet place at a time when you are safe from interruptions. Think of an important management risk you would like to pursue— something that is within your control but that you are afraid to initiate. Then answer each of the following questions:

- What are the detailed specifics of your management risk?

- What appeals to you about taking this risk?

- What will you gain from it, objectively and psychologically?

- What is frightening about the risk?

- What holds you back from taking it, and what do you stand to lose?

- What is the worst thing that can happen if you took the risk and it turned out badly?

- If the worst thing happens, then what can you do?

- If you need information to pursue this risk, where can you go for it?

- From whom can you get support?

- What can you do to make this risk less risky?

- What kinds of measures can you build in to make it less urgent, irreversible, or overwhelming?

- What aspect of your own style of making risky decisions do you need to allow or correct for in taking this risk?

- Suppose you break this risk into small steps:
  — What will be the first step? How soon can you take it?
  — What will be the second step? How soon can you take it?

- Sometimes you can help commit yourself to a course of action if you tell someone about your plan. What person can you tell about this fantasy to make it more real? Pick someone trustworthy, supportive, and open-minded.

CREDIT ACTUAL RISKING

We tend to discount the extent to which we take risks. If you undervalue the skills you have, you also undermine your confidence in improving them. It is important to remove this barrier by recognizing the risks you actually take.

You rob yourself of zeal and assertiveness by underrating the risks that are easy for you. Think about the tasks you perform smoothly but take for granted—functions you handle with ease but others find too risky to contemplate. Then acknowledge how much of a risk taker you really are; credit yourself for your "easy" risks.

Avoid the trap of rating yourself only according to risks that are too intimidating. Some managers assume the only risks that count are dramatic, gamble-with-the-company ones. In actuality, these daredevil risks happen rarely, and judging yourself on the basis of them gives a false picture of your aptitude and ability.

Another way you may slow your growth is by becoming obsessed with risks you haven't taken. You remember them vividly while ignoring the ones you take on a routine basis. Instead, acknowledge and appreciate what you have already accomplished. It will help boost the confidence you will need to handle risks you thought you would never attempt.

Respect the skills you already possess, looking for ways to stretch them. It is much easier to extend existing skills than to fashion them from scratch. That is why seeing yourself as a reasonable, effective risk taker enables you to continually improve yourself as one.

REDEFINE COURAGE

You will encounter risks only a naive manager could react to with anything but dismay—risks that would prompt the most competent and savvy manager to throw up her hands and walk away from an obviously hopeless situation. Senior executives face these circumstances with increasing frequency but without the luxury of being able to ignore them. An obstinately recessionary economy alone, for example, forces such difficult actions as laying off thousands of employees and shutting down facilities. Risks of this magnitude call for a new definition of management courage.

The kind of courage needed to take risks is simply "the capacity to move ahead *in spite of despair*" (May, 1975, p. 3). This version of courage endows you with the determination to risk in spite of pessimism or despondency. You allow yourself to feel afraid as you act in spite of your fears.

This brand of courage can take many forms: risking when you believe it is the right thing to do (moral courage); risking in spite of angry opposition from powerful colleagues (social courage); risking public mockery for unconventional ideas that could achieve major breakthroughs (creative courage); expressing personal feelings, convictions, or values in support of your risk (emotional courage); or challenging "sacred cow" principles, methods, or strategies in your work or organization (intellectual courage).

Management consultant Leeda Marting (1993) embraces new activities in which she lacks previous experience. "I'm drawn to new things, instead of just doing what I've done in the past. To me, risk taking means moving out against fear even though you are afraid of confronting it."

Marting practices this philosophy. She and a partner attempted to set up a venture capital fund concentrated exclusively in the communications industry. To their knowledge, they were the first women to attempt this. They raised more that $7 million, about half the minimum they needed. What sabotaged their immense effort was the reluctance of fund investors to trust Marting and her partner's ability to do what had not been done before. Time has proven these investors wrong, as similar funds now exist.

The more you allow yourself to attempt risks in spite of fear, the more you strengthen your mettle and tenacity. You don't have to be a superhero. You do need to move forward against formidable odds, knowing that true courage means acting despite constant misgivings.

This kind of courage resolves a paradox created by the necessary mixture of conviction and doubt in risk taking. Both believing and disbelieving in the risk is not only normal but also essential for proceeding responsibly. Managers claiming to be absolutely right pursue reckless courses of action that imperil themselves, their associates, the organization, and their customers or clients. They are blocked from accepting and acting on information that challenges their rigid beliefs.

Those who admit their doubts openly, yet risk in spite of them, acquire greater credibility, support, and forgiveness. And, in most cases, openly skeptical managers end up being more successful than their excessively self-assured peers.

RISK ANYWAY

To "risk anyway" means the following: you do it in spite of reservations and hesitation; having considered the dangers sufficiently, you proceed anyway. It also means taking a concrete step forward in the risk-taking process. Unless you move from the notion of learning to the motion of acting, you will remain stuck at your present level.

You learn to risk by doing it. Period. That is how others developed the skill. And before you dismiss it as simplistic and obvious, realize that this conclusion is supported by extensive research (Yates, 1992; Marone, 1992).

Action improves your skill because it creates change. And changing is a powerful way of learning. If you take a risk, you increase your knowledge and change your perspective and attitude toward it.

Action offers you the ultimate educational experience. You learn to risk by motion, deed, and exertion. Risk taking is a skill for participants, not for spectators. You think, plan, and practice on the ground. But to become a master you finally have to step out onto the risk highwire, the one stretching above heights of comfort and safety.

FOSTER RISK TAKING IN OTHERS

> I'm convinced that many companies flounder . . .
> because their people fail to see the company as a
> community of risk takers. In their minds . . . and in
> their methods . . . they've created a department of
> risk—in which the only risk-takers are the ones
> who eat in the executive dining room.
>
> —C. J. Silas

Cultivating your own risk mastery puts you in a position
to have a positive influence on the risk taking of others.
Overcoming one or two of your own risk barriers gives
you the experience to be an effective and empathetic sup-
porter of their struggles. Your responsible and assertive
behavior serves as a model for other employees, inspiring
them to risk similarly. Becoming an earnest and studious
apprentice of risk mastery will prepare you for the next
step: nurturing the risk taking of others.

MOVE RESPONSIBILITY
DOWN THE LINE

The art of management leadership includes supporting
other managers and employees in responsible risk-

taking. The numerous benefits of doing so include expanded decision-making resources, as well as potentially greater gains from increased risking. The alternatives to "delegating risk downward" are either taking them on yourself or seeking fewer and smaller risks.

Generally speaking, much of the risking gets passed up the line to senior managers, along with its privileges and liabilities (MacCrimmon and Wehrung, 1986). Some senior managers gladly share major risk decisions with employees one or several levels down the management hierarchy. Others reject the idea as impractical, complaining of the excessive risks foisted upon them, yet defending their prerogative to act. The more critical the risk, the more they feel obligated to make the decisions themselves. But even though certain management risks must always be made at senior levels, far more can be moved downward than typically assumed.

Passing up opportunities to delegate risks downward ensures that the decision-making skills of lower-level managers will remain at existing levels. On the other hand, allowing other managers and employees to risk will create effective learning experiences in which they can gain first-hand knowledge of the burdens that risk decision makers carry.

Delegating risk downward challenges you to gradually entrust those reporting to you with larger and more frequent risk decisions. By doing so, you aid and abet their managerial development, especially when they would avoid making decisions without your sponsorship or encouragement. Gradually elevating the level of their responsible risk taking helps you to minimize the price and maximize the profits of risk nurturing.

Their success, in turn, increases their own effectiveness, secures you the gains of the risks, and expands your staff resources for future risks. Their failure still develops their skills and your resources, but at a modest price for everyone, both financially and psychologically (Campbell, 1983).

Try this tactic on a small scale first. Start with the most competent employees reporting to you. Stretch your trust limits, as well as your willingness to transfer the control over risks. Even though some delegated risks will go amiss, you have demonstrated trust in your employees' potential for growth. Stand by them without complaining when their risks fail. Remember: what you learn from a risk failure may prove to be worth more in the long term than what you would have gained today from its success.

SHOW GREATER TRUST

You build the trust others need in order to develop their risk-taking skills by demonstrating your reliance on their integrity and ability. In other words, you build trust when you act in trusting ways. In order for others to believe they are trusted to initiate risks, their fears of unfair penalties for failure must be alleviated. When you eliminate such fears, you remove one of the most impenetrable barriers to risk learning.

Federal Express founder Frederick Smith is one prominent and successful CEO who puts this principle into practice, and his employees believe in him for it. The *Managers Guide* at Federal Express states that "Fear of failure must never be a reason not to try something different" (Labich, 1988b). Managers and employees at Federal Express are given fairly clear guidelines on the boundaries and conditions of their risk taking, and they know they are trusted to risk responsibly. According to Dave Rebhotz, vice president of customer service, they "feel very sure when they take a risk, there's minimal consequence to them" (Schlossberg, 1991, p. 6). Federal Express has demonstrated that risk taking and excep-

tional quality, performance, and profits can all work together. Evidence of this comes from their passing the
intense scrutiny of the examiners of the Malcolm Baldrige National Award for Quality with prize-winning
marks.

A number of actions can demonstrate your confidence in the ability of other managers and employees to
improve their risk-taking skills: verify whether they feel
ready for the risk assignment; ask them how you can
best support their management of the risk; resist the
well-meaning tendency to snoop (instead, have informal,
face-to-face update sessions); encourage them to ask for
help whenever they need it; allow them to handle the
risk their way, unless this sets them up to fail in ways
you find unaffordable or that are detrimental to them;
require them to keep notes on the "do's and don'ts" they
learned from the risk experience; and keep your word
about not punishing them when they have done their
best under the circumstances, regardless of the way the
risk turns out.

Other managers and employees feel trusted to pro-
pose new and larger risks, even though they may sound
like wild ideas, when they know senior management will
react to them respectfully. Peter Drucker (1974) argues
that senior managers should use their veto power subtly.
He recommends they first listen open-mindedly to bla-
tantly impractical ideas, then judge whether they can be
converted into useful ones. Drucker encourages senior
managers to continuously ask, "How would this idea
have to change to be practical, realistic, effective?" Risk-
nurturing senior managers recognize that it takes many
unworkable ideas to spawn one viable one. Genuinely
silly (stroke-of-insanity) and genuinely sensible (stroke-
of-genius) risks often seem equally absurd when first
articulated.

You also earn the trust essential to cultivating risk
mastery by telling others your risk-taking ground rules

clearly. Let them know when they change. Act in a manner that is 100 percent consistent with these rules.

In communicating your expectations, be careful to avoid sending mixed, catch-22 messages like this: you are supposed to take risks, but they should always succeed; you will look smart if a risk succeeds but dumb if it fails (no matter how well you managed it); you are supposed to predict outcomes before risking, even though they are inherently unpredictable; and you should take small risks but achieve big gains (an impossibility about 99 percent of the time).

Resist the tendency to judge others' risk-choosing patterns in relation to your own. In one study, managers were likely to rate managers higher whose attitudes toward risk were resembled their own. When risk-averse individuals are called upon to rate performance, the tendency could cause those whose performance is being rated to lose important pay or promotional opportunities (Grigsby and Leap, 1982, pp. 1139–1147).

Another way to demonstrate trust is through empowerment; that is, by supporting the "accountable freedom" of all staff members. It means they are free to take risks, for example, but should expect to be held accountable for their consequences. Not all managers want to empower their staff, and not all staff members want to be empowered. Yet the net benefits and practical payoffs of properly managed empowerment can be significant, especially in terms of building the trust between managers and employees essential for engaging in voluntary risk taking.

While the context is distant from the world of most managers, the empowerment experience of Stanford Business School lecturer Jim Collins illustrates how this trust-developing tactic can work in almost any situation, even among administrators and faculty in one of the nation's top business schools. "Without intending to toot my own horn, that's just what Stanford's business school deans did when they hired me as a faculty member. They took a risk on my abilities, drive, and potential, despite my lack of traditional academic qualifications. If I failed, the deans and the faculty would suffer unpleasant consequences. But they gave me a shot at teaching in a highly empowering kind of way. They simply trusted me, completely, to be able to do the job right. No one looked over my shoulder. Fortunately, this empowering risk paid off for everyone, including the dean, the faculty, and students" (1992). Collins received the Business School's Distinguished Teaching Award in 1992, making him the only faculty member to be recognized with a teaching award four times.

Jim Collins believes that managers need to take more risks in terms of empowering others. This means trusting them with greater freedom and autonomy, even though they may not live up to expectations.

REWARD LEARNING, NOT JUST OUTCOMES

Managers too often limit success criteria to whether the performance fulfills all intended goals. This undervalues a well-proven method of developing skills like risk taking: that of crediting how much your staff learned, regardless of how well they performed.

Studies of motivation and persistence confirm the advantages of learning goals over performance goals in skill development (Dweck, 1986). Performance goals push you to earn favorable judgments of the performance (or evade unfavorable ones); learning goals impel you to master a new task or increase skill competency (Marone, 1992). You can apply these findings to your risk development strategy by rewarding valued managers and employees for learning from risk taking, not just for successful outcomes from it.

Reward Learning from Unsuccessful Risks

The widespread practice of rewarding only success discourages learning among those afraid to risk or who have failed. These risk candidates require forbearance with regard to their mistakes as well as appreciation of their smallest successes. Ignoring them limits you to the current, perhaps small, pool of risk takers in your unit.

Every responsibly taken risk should be rewarded in some way, regardless of the outcome, if your aim is to stimulate learning among managers and employees. If this strikes you as naive, consider how an exclusively success-based reward policy might dampen increased and improved risk taking below the senior management level. Lower-level managers cannot be expected to take greater risks if events beyond human control deprive them of the credit for an otherwise outstanding performance.

Determining what constitutes an appropriate or proportionate learning reward is not a matter that can be standardized. You will need to match the specific reward with the specific risk in a specific circumstance. To assist you in this, here are some criteria you may want to consider using: the size of the risk; its difficulty; its current and long-term net gains; its relative importance for the unit or organization; the effort, commitment, and accountability demonstrated; the amount of growth demanded of the risk taker; and the size of the obstacles overcome to implement the risk. In other words, make the reward commensurate with the risk and the outcome.

When rewarding so-called risk failure, communicate clearly what is being recognized: the effort, the planning, the learning, and so forth. If the unsuccessful risk was irresponsibly undertaken, of course, it may deserve some kind and measure of penalty, instead of reward.

Reward Learning from Successful Risks

Risk takers generally receive too little recognition for their success. Being allowed the chance to risk again is one common reward, and while it does motivate continued risk taking and learning, especially for advanced risk takers, it is sufficient only for the few managers and employees willing to risk on a larger scale or more frequently by their own free choice. A routine slap on the back is hardly enough for an employee exposed to the increased hazards of voluntary risk taking—the kind of risking that often leads to greater success.

By compensating appropriately, you give a clear signal that you are committed to others taking elective, but responsible, risks. When they see success in doing so rewarded generously, they will recalculate the payoffs for becoming more assertive, frequent, and ambitious risk takers. When this kind of risk taking becomes a prerequisite for rewards like bigger budgets, bigger projects, better perks, or faster promotions, most people will be looking more favorably on the voluntary risks they now automatically dismiss.

Sharing financial gains can generate high managerial and organizational dividends. Some corporations, in fact, share the benefits of risk investments with managers in order to keep innovators on board. Others do not. Richard Branson, CEO of the Virgin Group, believes many corporations are greedy about how they share the benefits of risk taking, and that those firms lose far more than they presume they save with this policy. His British conglomerate operates differently. "We in the Virgin Group are often seemingly very liberal with the way we give managers minority share holdings and participation in new ventures in new markets . . . people within the company who are capable of becoming millionaires if they set up on their own are people we want to stick with the company and become millionaires" (Branson, 1985, pp. 7–8).

USE CREATIVE INCENTIVES

While traditional rewards such as bonuses work well, creative incentives have additional risk promoting qualities. They inspire more immediate action and greater exertion, and can motivate more forcefully. Consistent risk takers find special incentives more meaningful than conventional rewards. Studies confirm their willingness "to have a greater proportion of their total compensation in incentive plans" (Grey, 1978, p. 12). Given the choice, the risk-oriented manager, for instance, prefers a higher salary potential over a lower salary guarantee.

Incentives offer several comparative advantages over routine rewards like the kind given at annual banquets or picnics. Incentives can be customized easily to the personality of the risk taker or the nature of the risk. They can be quickly arranged and presented, meaning that the recipient does not have to wait for eleven months to enjoy it. And you, rather than someone above you, can choose the incentive's timing, size, and form.

As emphasized with rewards, fit the risk-learning incentive to the person, the risk, and the organizational culture. At Apple Computer, well-known for its aggressive, risk-taking culture, people pick the rewards for outstanding performance from a large pool of options chosen by fellow employees. You can bet these options reflect the kind of people working at Apple.

A small and less known high technology company has developed its own version of Apple's approach (Dunnaway, 1992). This company uses "recognition coupons" to reward initiative and innovation at all organizational levels. All employees receive blank coupons that they can award to anyone, completely at their own discretion. To use the coupons, they write their name on the coupon and name the recipient and her or his actions.

Award recipients redeem the recognition coupons at any time for company-donated prizes, which range from home electronic appliances to hotel stays. Bigger awards require more coupons.

Even if this system does not stress risk taking per se, it invites and reinforces it at all organizational levels. The recognition coupons promote risk-related actions, like enterprise and ingenuity. And they produce risk-related benefits, like breakthroughs in productivity and profits. Note management's own risk taking in trusting employee decision making and respecting employee integrity with this unconventional recognition system.

There is no limit to the range of your incentive options, except for that of your imagination and budget. Tell your employees what a great job they did. Award them certificates exchangeable for anything from entertainment to electronic status symbols (like the latest portable cellular telephone). Allow them extra days off or a weekend vacation at company expense in connection with out-of-town business travel. As fits your personality and theirs, create humorous incentives, such as a Turtle of the Month Award for employees who stick their necks out, or a customized T-shirt or sweatshirt. And, of course, you can always give them a custom-worded plaque or some other kind of meaningful memento.

PROVIDE
ADEQUATE RESOURCES

To further motivate manager and employee risk learning, make sure they receive sufficient resources. Assure them they will be supplied with adequate scheduling, research and information, staffing, money, and training.

Scheduling

Authorizing the added time necessary to take risks responsibly will pay a double dividend. It demonstrates management's commitment to supporting responsible risk takers and at the same time enhances the chances of their success. More time to research and plan the risk, for example, helps to reduce its dangers. No one assumes this will be easy for increasingly budget constrained organizations. But to the extent that you can, and whenever you can, free risk takers from low-priority, routine tasks that can be delegated to others, even if only temporarily.

Information

Underwrite and make available any research—particularly internal information—that supports responsible risk taking. Eliminate any bureaucratic red tape blocking timely access to information deemed absolutely essential for the risk to succeed. In the view of a former president of Dow Chemical Europe, management has an obligation to support or secure this information. "To those who should take risks the company owes the best in data gathering systems, the analytical capabilities that are required and total support during decision making and the all-important execution phase of the undertaking" (Clutterbuck, 1982, p. 13).

Staffing

Make available the additional human talent needed to pursue responsible risks. Ask other managers if current work loads or delivery schedules can be adjusted to free up the needed personnel. Review work plans with an eye on ways to do the same job faster. Solicit volunteers willing to put in their own time to share in the risk, and inform them of their right to responsible-risk rewards. Beg, borrow, or barter to procure the human resources necessary for a successful risk.

Money

Risk taking requires proper funding. Yet as more and more managers grapple with budget cuts, the notion of spending money on optional risks may be attractive but unrealistic. So how do you defend the need to spend money on voluntary risks? Depending on the extent of your current fiscal crisis, you may not have any choice.

No matter how desperate your budget situation, give some thought to answering these questions before dismissing new risk initiatives: Without taking risks, how can your managers and employees possibly apply and improve their risk skills? Can you afford not to risk at this time? Is it ever easy to invest in risky ideas? The gains from risking often mean more in difficult than in good financial times. What assurance do you have that not risking will prove the wisest action? Before giving up in despair over current spending embargoes, reflect on whether it is worse to invest or not invest in risks that may or may not solve problems.

If your current budget is not so constrained (or when it improves), you can more easily underwrite the costs of voluntary risks. Doing so sends a persuasive message. You trust and expect managers and staff to learn by actually risking. The amount need not be excessive, but it should be adequate.

Risk takers should be held fully accountable for funds allocated to them. Require them to personally report their use of the funds to a senior manager, and the president or CEO if possible, regardless of the outcome of the risk. This report should include specific lessons learned and recommendations on how to profit from them, if possible, both immediately and in the long term.

If the required financial resources cannot be secured, postpone or cancel the risk. Inadequately supported ventures stand little chance of success and cannot be considered responsible risk taking. Another reason to spurn them is the potential backlash they can trigger, reducing the willingness to risk in the future.

Risk learners need flexibility in managing their financial resources. Overly strict controls will undermine and complicate effective risk management. Peter Drucker suggests using budgetary controls that are different from those appropriate for ongoing business (Drucker, 1974).

One more suggestion: earmark a nominal amount of your own or another's annual budget for risk taking. You may want to set this up as a separate, use-it-or-lose-it, risk venture fund. Set a fixed percentage of every manager's budget, depending on what you can afford and the actual dollar amounts at stake.

Setting aside some reserves, however difficult, can be managed from time to time. Rebecca Klemm, president of her own six-year-old research firm, has more control over this option than most corporate managers. Her first-hand experience with it, however, offers instruction in the practicalities of both creating and using a risk-taking reserve fund.

> One reason I can take more risks than most executives is that I make sure I have the financial reserves to survive them if they fail. It's always tempting to spend that reserve on other enticing business opportunities. But I force myself to put some money into my risk-taking reserves every year. In a big corporation, of course, top management would take those reserves away from me. But

in this company, I'm the chief financial officer as well as the president.

Last year was our worst ever financially. I used those reserves to keep us going during a long business drought. Believe me, that was probably the biggest risk I've ever taken. I was really scared to use those reserves, especially as we used them to take bigger-than-ever business risks just to stay in business during recessionary times.

I know I could have lost it all, but if I hadn't used our reserves, we wouldn't be in business today. I guess I'm saying not only do you have to risk putting aside a reserve account to survive special and routine business risks, but you have to take the more frightening risk of using it when the time comes [Klemm, 1992].

Training

Training strengthens risk-seeking knowledge. When followed by on-the-job application and reinforcement, it also builds and sharpens the necessary practical skills. Training must be implemented competently to nurture skills and abilities that are consistent with the organization's mission.

The best results from training occur when it is properly structured. The program should include a customized training design; highly qualified trainers with indepth expertise in both the content and the process of risk training; an assessment of participants' needs and concerns; case examples of your organization's risks; more than one training session, with enough time between sessions to practice on the job; and confidential, one-on-one, post-training coaching for participants.

Even if you can't satisfy all of these criteria, make sure you and fellow managers do three things, no matter what: participate in the training early on; apply and model the training in your own work; and remove management-related obstacles to participants' practicing what they learned.

One-on-One Support

Individualized, intangible support is just as vital as material resources to nurturing others' risk taking. Examples: encouraging others to take new or larger risks; expressing confidence in their ability to manage unexpected setbacks and problems; offering to back others up if the risk fails (and was responsibly taken); and showing genuine interest in and support of others' efforts to achieve risk mastery. Although such one-on-one support saves money, it does cost time, an equally rare commodity in most organizations.

Here are additional ways managers can give one-on-one risk-learning support: encourage others to talk candidly about their risks, including their problems and concerns; reassure them of no reprisals for unanticipated or unpreventable risk losses; expand their risk decision boundaries at a comfortable pace; and serve as a shield or buffer for employees when the organizational culture runs counter to their risk taking. Risk takers need to believe they are not alone in their venture (Sisson, 1986). They also need to believe they will still have your support if the venture does not work out.

DEVELOP
WRITTEN GUIDELINES

Few organizations have clearly defined risk-taking guidelines, and perhaps none have written ones. The risk attitudes of boards of directors, for example, are generally unarticulated in any explicit way. "Even corporations with centralized management teams, strategic plans, and management information systems to support

decision making lack centralized policies for risk seeking," notes management consultant John Cozzolino
(1982, p. 42). That absence of explicitly communicated
guidelines suppresses and restricts responsible risk taking at all organizational levels.

Senior management should invest exceptional
thought and effort in drafting formal risk-taking policies. They need to give careful thought, for instance, to
the following: Are these policies consistent with the organization's vision and values? Do they spell out the
risks each employee may autonomously take and under
what conditions? Do they define what factors make a
risk "responsible" or "acceptable," regardless of the outcome? Do they encourage and support this kind of risk
taking? Is there a process for updating employees on
changes in these policies?

Senior management should also pay extra attention
to necessary differences in risk-taking policy for each
functional area. This involves identifying areas that
need a high degree of risk initiating and areas where it
is not needed or may be damaging. Take the marketing
department, for instance. It may require supplementary
guidelines on risk taking. Try to determine what kinds
of risks would be too big to take and what kinds would
be acceptable. Try to document precisely the conditions
under which certain risks may be taken (Green, 1969).
You can even go as far as attempting to define tolerable
amounts of uncertainty. Allowing different departments
to adapt specific policies and performance criteria will
open up avenues for innovation. The research and development division, for example, may need greater risk-
taking freedom than the customer relations department.

Given these considerations, senior management has
compelling reasons to do what it takes to produce sensible, workable, and understandable risk-taking policies. These policies mark the bases and foul lines of the
risk ballpark. They define the organizationwide rules of

responsible risk taking. Given their scope and impact, senior management will need to develop and communicate them with the same care given any new policy.

FORM RISK TEAMS

Organize teams to initiate and pursue risks. Few experiences cement the bond between employees more than going through large-scale risks together. Consider the alliances that troops form during military operations. Similarly, a camaraderie develops among employees while battling management risks (Collins, 1992). The ideal is for team members to have a strong commitment to ensuring the success of the risk.

These teams function best when operating much like quality improvement teams. To start with, put the team's risk-taking purpose and boundaries in writing. Review and clarify this charter with them in person. Select team members from all units that have a stake in the outcome. Appoint a manager, and give that person the authority to remove internal barriers to leading the team. Require them to gather data as they develop the plan and strategy; insist that decisions reflect, but not be limited by, their own or anyone else's data. Consider using an outside professional facilitator to enhance the team's productivity and performance, unless one of the members has expertise in group dynamics and team building.

MIX SEEKERS
AND AVOIDERS

You nurture risk taking more systematically when you create a mixture of risk takers and risk avoiders. Too much chance taking can endanger an organization's need for stability and continuity. Likewise, too much risk avoidance can threaten an organization's need for innovation and change. One way of attaining and maintaining this balance is by paying close attention to the proportion of risk-inclined and risk-averse staff.

No precise formula exists for calculating the best mix. In the absence of a proven ideal ratio of risk takers to risk avoiders, answering the following questions may help establish a rough equilibrium between risking and not risking in any organization (Grey and Gordon, 1978, pp. 8–13):

- Is your organization developing or mature? If it is still evolving, it will need a greater number of risk initiators.

- Is it capital- or people-intensive? The more capital-intensive it is, the fewer risk initiators it needs.

- Are your organization's goals ambitious, moderate, or conservative? The more aspiring and audacious the objectives are, the more risk initiators the organization will need.

- Is your organization high- or low-technology-dependent? The more technology-dependent the organization, the more risk initiators it will need.

- To what extent are your managers rewarded with bonuses or other incentive plans in addition to their base salaries? The more incentive-oriented your organization, the more risk initiators it will need.

- Is your organization's track record of new products, services, and programs outstanding, average, or below average? The less outstanding the performance record, the more risk initiators it will need.

- Is your organization's resistance to change and innovation high, medium, or low, compared to the other successful organizations in the field? The stronger the resistance to change, the more risk choosers the organization will need.

As the questions imply, having the right number of risk takers, as well as the right amount of risk taking, requires knowing the dimensions of your organization's strategy for long-term survival and success.

It also requires feeling comfortable hiring people of differing aptitudes and abilities. Research confirms that risk-inclined managers select risk-inclined employees and, equally consistently, risk-averse managers prefer to hire risk-averse employees (Grey and Gordon, 1978). A decision to hire people with or without strong risk-taking skills, and with or without proven track records, requires surmounting the tendency to hire people like oneself. This is a high hurdle for most managers to leap, in the experience of executive search consultant Leeda Marting (1993). Too many managers, she finds, hire people who replicate their own beliefs and behavior. She rarely finds a client asking for an executive with a background much different from current managers, and this includes a candidate's risk-taking track record.

Detecting a candidate's risk-seeking skills during interviews can be difficult. In fact, while being interviewed, managers report they take more risks than they eventually do once hired (MacCrimmon and Wehrung, 1986). Ask job candidates about the details of previous risks they have taken. Probe for signs of their risk-seeking competency and drive. It will help immensely to use the self-assessment tools from Chapter Three during interviews.

CROSS THE RISK BARRIER

These risk-fostering tactics can work in any environment, even in government agencies or nonprofit institutions, where getting people to take risks is even more difficult than in the private sector. The rewards for risk taking in a nonprofit setting like a large state university, observes James Madison University president Ronald Carrier, differ from those in the private sector: "When you take risks in the public sector, the rewards are mostly psychic and personal, such as the satisfaction of doing something right for those served by your agency or institution" (1992). Carrier uses a time-tested formula to spark risk taking among tenured and other security-oriented employees. He sets brass rings of self-esteem, self-challenge, and self-respect high on a wall of uncertainty and risk. He then tosses a challenge over the wall and invites them to climb over and retrieve it. Carrier gives employees meaningful and satisfying reasons to take new risks when they could just as easily stay on the all-too-familiar safe side of the wall.

In the many dozens of instances reported recently in *Reinventing Government* (Osborne and Gaebler, 1992), the payoffs of risk-taking in that sector have been enormous. Government managers generally succeed less because of their achievements and more by not doing anything wrong. Yet a sizable number are taking risks in making their agencies more decentralized, more entrepreneurial, and more responsive.

In a recent issue of *Governing* (Sylvester, 1992, pp. 46–50), it was reported that a growing number of government managers are finding ways to create work cultures that encourage more risk taking. They make the following suggestions:

- Rely on goals and values, and not on procedures, to find innovative solutions to traditional problems.

- Search out risk takers by asking people about their risks and how they recovered from the ones that failed.

- Take the suggestion box seriously and evaluate all ideas respectfully.

- Make public heroes of those who accept responsibility, and celebrate their risk effort with parties, small prizes, or any sincere form of recognition.

- Encourage risk takers to keep trying despite failures by blaming the idea, not them, and by valuing what was learned.

- Head off the critics by being forthcoming with your failure and stressing what was done to lessen the chances and costs of the risk failing.

If business is willing to learn from government, these guidelines can foster risk taking even in the most risk-inhibiting environment.

LINK THE THREE TRIANGLES OF RISK

A last, "super" tactic condenses many of the risk-taking methods in *Highwire Management*. Figure 10.1 illustrates this tactic's integrative and simplifying elements. These features make this approach applicable to any manager and any risk in any circumstance. Properly used by the right team of managers and employees, the triangles offer a framework for developing risk-taking policies and guidelines for any work group.

The outer triangle shows the three views of risk taking that undergird *Highwire Management*: *management philosophy*, or your fundamental beliefs about risks, such as the risks of not risking; *management practices*, or your risk behavior and procedures, such as framing risk decisions in terms of gains, not just losses; and *management strategy*, or your vision, plan, and

Figure 10.1. Triple Triangle of Management Risk Taking.

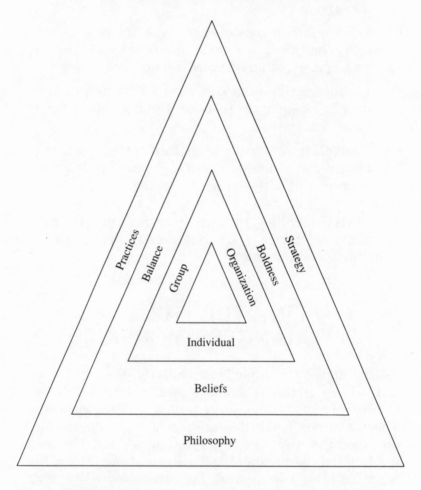

methods for achieving organizational or divisional goals, such as viewing your risk taking as primarily a long-term management strategy.

The middle triangle contains the three core tactical elements of risk taking: beliefs, balance, and boldness. *Beliefs* refers to your risk-taking principles. Do you believe risk taking is an acquired skill? Do you believe today's environment requires more risk taking than previously? *Balance* refers to the pragmatic weighing and adjusting of the pros and cons of the risk. Are the potential gains sufficient to justify potential losses? *Boldness* refers to the assertive and self-initiating quality of your risk behavior. Do you have the audacity to take the unreasonable risk actions reasonable managers will generally condemn or ridicule? To stand the best chance of succeeding, any risk tactic should incorporate deeply held beliefs, a reasonable balance of practical considerations, and dynamic boldness in both vision and action.

The inner triangle separates the risk into three domains: the *individual*, or the person leading the risk taking; the *group*, or the work unit or group most directly or intensively involved in taking the risk, whether a permanent group or an ad hoc one; and the *organization*, or obviously, the entire organization.

Applying the three triangles to any risk, your own or others, involves two steps: first, examining the risk using each of the three triangles separately; second, fusing the three analyses by identifying interactions among the triangles. In other words, scrutinize the risk within each triangle and then between each triangle.

In applying these steps to the risk of implementing total quality management (TQM) organizationwide, for example, consider first its risk dimensions, the outer triangle. How well does your management risk philosophy support such a revolutionary change in the work culture? Is it sufficiently pro-risk taking that a large majority of managers will back TQM? Ask similar questions about your management practices (are your risk-taking skills adequate for TQM risk?) and your management strategy (can you risk an organizational change lasting three to five years, at a minimum?).

Next, evaluate the TQM risk using the middle triangle. What beliefs within your organization could thwart TQM, such as skepticism about its faddishness?

What balance in practical matters will TQM implementation involve? What, for instance, are the tradeoff risks of allocating scarce time and resources to TQM rather than to other projects? Will enough managers and employees change their own behavior despite vigorous personal resistance to any TQM notions they dispute, like empowering all employees? The last element in the tactical triangle, boldness, assesses individual and collective courage. Are top managers genuinely and courageously committed to implementing TQM, despite its risk qualities (uncertainty, gains, losses, and significance)?

If you link all three triangles, you cover all of your risk-taking bases in a feasible and pragmatic manner. In the absence of unlimited human, fiscal, and material resources, the triangles enable you to evaluate risks sufficiently, if not exhaustively. In the absence of an orderly, predictable, or rational world, they enable you to make fully competent, if not always precisely correct, risk decisions. And in the absence of work cultures that reward risk taking, they enable you to risk responsibly, if not without criticism or consequences.

Having expanded your risk resources . . . having challenged your risk attitudes . . . having updated your risk expertise . . . having assessed your risk skills . . . and having gained whatever else this book offered or inspired, your next action is clear: to walk the risk highwire with conviction, mastery, and courage.

Appendix: Research Notes

The information on which this book is based comes from the following sources:

- The research and analysis of university scholars from diverse disciplines: psychology, management, sociology, philosophy, statistics, and economics.

- The risk-taking research and analysis of nonacademic experts: managers, consultants, journalists, and other writers.

- The first-hand risk-taking experiences and insights of managers I interviewed for the book

- Case studies of management risk taking from various types of publications, including newspapers, business magazines, business school journals, and novels.

- My own risk-taking observations, experiences, and expertise as a manager, trainer, and consultant. Most of the tactics in this book have been tested by participants in my risk-taking seminars over the last three years.

To make reading easier, certain technical details related to the research cited in the book are omitted. These include descriptions of such information as the population used for a given study, the specific risk-taking instruments and measures used, the research design, the statistical limitations of the data, and so on. Readers should be assured, however, that only scientifically sound research and the viewpoints of widely respected risk experts are reported.

Those wanting detailed information about research sources or methodological aspects of research on risk-taking behavior should consult the bibliography, and the following sources in particular: Dawes, 1988; MacCrimmon and Wehrung, 1986; Marone, 1992; Siegelman, 1983; and Yates, 1992.

The following executives and managers were interviewed by the author during 1991 and 1992. They have a wide range of management positions and backgrounds and represent all types and sizes of organizations. In the interviews they were asked to talk informally and candidly about their management risk-taking beliefs, experiences, and advice. Their responses are quoted in *Highwire Management* as I have interpreted and edited them. Thanks to these forthright people, the tools and tactics of management risk taking come alive for the reader's benefit.

Ronald Carrier, President, James Madison University (JMU). Carrier has been president of JMU (rated one of the best undergraduate public colleges in America) since 1971. He is well known as an advocate of bold ideas in the generally risk-averse academic world. Recently, for example, he took a year's leave to direct a struggling state technology center that has since generated tens of millions of dollars in economic growth in Virginia. Carrier himself is a recipient of awards and honors for his leadership of innovative ventures few others would attempt.

Lowell Christy, Technology Management Consultant. Christy is a consultant on high technology policy for manufacturing and development in the United States and abroad. He directed the Technology and Innovation Management Center at Stanford Research Institute (SRI) and, early in his career, cofounded several technology firms involved in telecommunications software and high technology advertising products.

Jim Collins is coauthor of *Beyond Entrepreneurship: Turning Your Business into an Enduring Great Company* (1992). He is also recipient of the Distinguished Teaching Award at Stanford's Graduate School of Business, a management consultant, and an avid rock climber.

Richard Donnelly, Executive Director of the Executive M.B.A. Program and professor in the School of Business and Public Management, the George Washington University. Donnelly's teaching and research focus on technology innovation and entrepreneurship, project management, and the management of research and development. Outside of the university, he consults and leads training in both the private and federal sectors. Previously, he directed new product/new business development for a Fortune 50 firm in a worldwide business area.

Joyce Doria, Vice President, Human Resource Management, Booz-Allen & Hamilton. Doria developed a new consulting practice from a staff of three to more than fifty within three years at Booz-Allen. Lacking a suitable female role model for becoming a senior manager in an intensely competitive environment, Joyce became her own mentor and learned primarily from her own successes and failures. Her willingness to risk paid off when she became Booz-Allen's first female partner in the Worldwide Technology Center in 1988.

Ross Garber, Strategic Planning Manager, Epoch Systems. Epoch Systems was rated the eighteenth fastest growing high tech company in the United States by *Business Week* in December 1991. Garber manages strategic direction and relationships for the 170-person company, which sells systems management software for computer networks. He holds a B.A. degree in finance from the University of Massachusetts.

Laura Henderson, President and Founder, Prospect Associates. Henderson started a consulting firm specializing in supporting national health care planning more than four years ago. Her 150-person firm today provides a range of management technical services in health communications and biomedical research. Henderson is active in the National Association of Women Business Owners. In 1991 she was named a regional Women in Business Advocate of the Year by the U.S. Small Business Administration and in 1989 she received Arthur Young's Entrepreneur of the Year Award.

Carole Herod, Senior Vice President, Program Management and Planning, MCI Communications. With MCI since 1984, Herod is currently responsible for integrating the efforts of MCI's various technical development groups, focusing on new product delivery. In addition, she manages the technical planning, human resources, and quality management groups within MCI's Strategy and Technology organization. She has held a variety of corporate marketing, sales, and product management positions within MCI, such as product manager for 800 Service and MCI WATS. She has also held various sales and marketing management positions with AT&T and Sprint.

Arthur I. Hersh, President and CEO, Software Productivity Consortium. Hersh took over leadership of the Software Productivity Consortium in 1989 following a thirty-two-year career with GTE Government Systems. The Consortium develops improved processes and methods by which aerospace companies create and implement large software-intensive systems. He acts as the principal point of contact with member firms of the Consortium, such as the Boeing Company, Rockwell International, Lockheed, and Martin Marietta.

Jeanne Hollister, Vice President, Investor Relations, Aetna Life and Casualty. Hollister has held a variety of line and staff positions at Aetna. Prior to joining them over ten years ago, she worked for two years with Connecticut General (now Cigna). She is a fellow of the Casualty Actuarial Society and a member of the Corporate Advisory Board of the National Foundation of Women Business Owners. The mother of two young children, she has made more than one risky career trade-off while managing to balance her family and professional lives.

Peter Keen, Chairman, International Center for Information Technologies. Keen was named one of the top ten information technology consultants in the United States by *Information Week* in 1988. He recently authored *Shaping the Future: Business Design Through Information Technology* and advises senior managers of public and private organizations worldwide, including international airlines, financial service firms, petrochemical companies, and transnational corporations. He has written several books on business and telecommunications and teaches at Fordham University's Graduate School of Business Administration.

Rebecca Klemm, President, Klemm Analysis Group, Inc. Klemm's six-year-old firm conducts management and technical studies for commercial and government organizations in areas of public policy, health services, product liability, and statistical auditing. Previously, she taught for six years at the schools of Business Administration at Georgetown and Temple universities. She draws on her Ph.D. degree in statistics and her extensive research and publication experience during her frequent appearances as an expert witness in judicial and congressional proceedings.

Richard Lesher, President, U.S. Chamber of Commerce. Lesher has been president of America's largest business advocacy federation for almost twenty years. More than 215,000 companies are members of the U.S. Chamber of Commerce, along with 3,000 state and local chambers, 1,300 trade and professional associations, and 65 American chambers overseas. He writes a weekly syndicated column, "Voice of Business," which is carried by nearly 700 newspapers coast-to-coast. For more than twelve years, Lesher has appeared weekly on "It's Your Business," a public affairs debate program carried on more than 145 commercial television stations nationwide.

Leeda P. Marting, Independent Philanthropic Consultant and Senior Consultant, Boyden, Inc. Marting specializes in the management and governance of foundations and other nonprofit organizations. She served previously as Executive Director of the John Hay Whitney Foundation and Director of Contributions and Community Affairs at Levi Strauss. She has also worked extensively to help companies establish philanthropic and social responsibility programs.

William R. T. Oakes, President, Viar & Company. Oakes has been president of Viar, a professional services firm specializing in the federal sector, since 1988. He has been an investor in and key manager of several professional services and manufacturing companies, including Kappa Systems, a government consulting firm; Transpace Carriers, an unmanned space launch services firm;

and PMIC, a manufacturer of computer equipment components.

Charlotte Taylor, President, Venture Concepts. Taylor is the author of *Women in the Business Game; The Entrepreneurial Game: Strategies for Successful Ownership;* and *The Entrepreneurial Workbook: A Step by Step Guide to Starting a Business.* She is founder and owner of Venture Concepts, a fourteen-year-old, full-service management consulting firm that specializes in helping owner-managed firms from start-up and strategic planning through the entrepreneurial phase.

Ted Wiss, Vice President, Sales and Marketing, Potomac Digital. Wiss has over twenty years of experience in marketing high technology to Fortune 1,000 firms. In his present position he directs sales and marketing activities in the area of data communications systems.

Dona Wolf, Director, Human Resources Development Group, U.S. Office of Personnel Management (OPM). As a member of the elite Federal Senior Executive Service, Wolf oversees OPM's training programs for more than two million employees with a budget of more than $100 million earned through competition with other federal training programs and the private sector. Recently she spearheaded a ground-breaking revision of the government's training policies.

References

Acs, J. "A Comparison of Models for Strategic Planning, Risk Analysis, and Risk Management." *Theory and Decisions,* 1985, *19,* 205–248.

Adler, S. "Risk-Making Management." *Business Horizons,* Apr. 1980, pp. 11–14.

Albrecht, K. *The Only Thing That Matters.* New York: Harper Business, 1992.

Alexander, C. "Outplacement Blues." In S. E. Murphy, J. G. Sperling, and J. D. Sperling (eds.), *The Literature of Work.* Phoenix, Ariz.: University of Phoenix Press, 1991.

Alvarez, A. *The Armchair Mountaineer.* New York: Charles Scribner's Sons, 1984.

Anderson, R. M. "Handling Risk in Defense Contracting." *Harvard Business Review,* July/Aug. 1969, pp. 90–98.

Armstrong, S. "How Expert Are the Experts?" *INC,* Dec. 1981, pp. 15–16.

Arrow, K. "Risk Perception in Psychology and Economics." *Economic Inquiry,* Jan. 1982, pp. 1–9.

Athearn, J. L., Pritchett, S. T., and Schmit, J. T. *Risk and Insurance.* (6th ed.) St. Paul, Minn.: West Publishing Company, 1989.

Atkinson, J. "Motivational Determinants of Risk-Taking Behavior." *Psychological Review*, 1957, pp. 359–372.

Baird, I., and Thomas, H. "Toward a Contingency Model of Strategic Risk Taking." *Academy of Management Review*, 1985, *10*(2), 230–243.

Bazerman, M. H. *Judgment in Managerial Decision Making*. New York: Wiley, 1986.

Belovicz, M., and Finch, F. "A Critical Analysis of the 'Risky Shift' Phenomenon." *Organizational Behavior and Human Performance*, 1971, *6*, 150–168.

Bem, D. "The Concept of Risk in the Study of Human Behavior." In J. Dowie and P. LeFrere (eds.), *Risk and Chance: Selected Readings*. England: Open University Press, 1980.

Bennis, W. "Followers Make Good Leaders Good." *New York Times*, Dec. 31, 1989, p. F-3.

Bennis, W., and Nanus, B. *Leaders*. New York: Harper-Collins, 1985.

Betz, F. *Managing Technology*. Englewood Cliffs, N.J.: Prentice-Hall, 1987.

Blaylock, B. "Risk Perception: Evidence of an Interactive Process." *Journal of Business Research*, 1985, *13*, 207–221.

Block, P. *The Empowered Manager: Positive Political Skills at Work*. San Francisco: Jossey-Bass, 1988.

Block, P. "Enough Already with the Bottom Line." *Training*, Apr. 1988, pp. 97–99.

Blum, S. "Investment Preferences and the Desire for Security: A Comparison of Men and Women." *Journal of Psychology*, 1976, *94*, 87–91.

Booher, D. *The Competitive Edge—Publishing Your Ideas in Articles and Books*. Houston, Tex.: Booher Writing Consultants, 1985.

Bowman, E. "Risk Seeking by Troubled Firms." *Sloan Management Review*, Summer 1982, pp. 33–42.

Brannigan, M. "Costly Strategy: Southeast Banking Got

in Trouble by Sticking to Its Stodgy Ways." *Wall Street Journal,* Jan. 9, 1991, pp. A-1.

Branson, R. "Risk Taking." *Journal of General Management,* 1985, *11*(2), 5-11.

Brenner, R. *History—The Human Gamble.* Chicago: University of Chicago Press, 1983.

Bridges, E. "Effects of Hierarchical Differentiation on Group Productivity, Efficiency, and Risk Taking." *Administrative Science Quarterly,* pp. 305-319.

Broad, W. "High Risk of New Shuttle Disaster Leads NASA to Consider Options." *New York Times,* Apr. 9, 1989, pp. 1, 24.

Brown, W., and Swoboda, F. "At GM, New Team Shakes Up Culture from Top Down." *Washington Post,* Jan. 31, 1993, pp. H-1.

Burgess, J. "Fighting to Stay Fit." *Washington Post,* Nov. 15, 1990, pp. H-1.

Burnside, R. "Creativity, 'Jehtinho,' and Hindsight." *Issues and Observations,* Fall 1989, pp. 3-5.

Byrd, R. *A Guide to Personal Risk Taking.* New York: AMACOM, 1984.

Byrd, R. *The Creatrix Inventory.* San Diego, Calif.: University Association, 1986. (Originally published 1972.)

Camerer, C. F., and Kunreuther, H. "Decision Processes for Low Probability Events: Policy Implications." *Journal of Policy Analysis and Management,* 1989, *8,* 565-592.

Campbell, D. "How to Take Line Management Risks: Push Them Downward." *Issues and Observations,* 1983, pp. 5-6.

Carrier, R. Interview with the author, 1992.

Carroll, J. *Managing Risk: A Computer-Aided Strategy.* Stotteham, Mass.: Butterworths, 1984.

Chase, J. "Afternoon in America." *INC,* July 31, 1988, p. 31.

Christy, L. Interview with the author, 1992.

CIC Enterprises. *Body Bulletin, Are You Gutsy Enough?* Emmaus, Pa.: Rodale Press, 1988.

Clark, R. "Risk Taking in Groups: A Social Psychological Analysis." *Journal of Risk and Insurance,* 1991, pp. 75–92.

Clines, F. "A Master of Compromise Tapped for the Treasury." *New York Times,* Feb. 3, 1985, p. F-6.

Clutterbuck, D. "Are Today's Managers Risk-Shy?" *International Management,* May 1982, pp. 10–13.

Coates, J. "Why the People Are Scared." *Vital Speeches of the Day,* Oct. 1979, pp. 176–180.

Cohen, R. "The Creator of Time Warner, Steven J. Ross, Is Dead at 65." *New York Times,* Dec. 21, 1992, pp. 1, D-12.

Collins, J. "What It Takes to Be Creative." *Flashcourse Newsletter,* Winter 1987-88.

Collins, J. Interview with the author, 1992.

Collins, J. "On the Edge." *Stanford,* Dec. 1990, pp. 41–47.

Committee on Risk and Decision Making, Assembly of Behavioral and Social Sciences, National Research Council. *Risk and Decision Making: Perspectives and Research.* Washington, D.C.: National Academy Press, 1982.

"Companies Show a New Gusto for Risk-Taking." *International Management,* Dec. 1983, pp. 64–68.

"Complex Decisions: A Fine Mess You've Gotten Us into Now!" *Pryor Report,* Jan. 1986, p. 9.

Contavespi, V. "Tips from Winners in the Game of Wealth." *Forbes,* Oct. 22, 1990, pp. 32–38.

Cotton, P., and Harvey, G. "How to Create Creativity." *Management Today,* May 1984, pp. 74–77.

Cox, S. *Indirections: For Those Who Want to Write.* New York: Nonpareil Books, 1947.

Cozzolino, J. "How Much Risk Will Your Finance Committee Take?" *Directors and Boards,* Winter 1982, pp. 41–45.

Craig, D. *Native Stones: A Book About Climbing.* North Pomfret, Vt.: Secker, 1987.

Cummings, L., and others. "Risk, Fate, Conciliation, and Trust: An International Study of Attitudinal Differences Among Executives." *Academy of Management Journal,* Sept. 1971, pp. 285-304.

"The Customer Is Always Right." *Time,* Mar. 7, 1988, p. 57.

Dauw, D. C. *Up Your Career.* Prospect Heights, Ill.: Waveband Press, 1980.

Dawes, R. M. *Rational Choice in an Uncertain World.* San Diego, Calif.: Harcourt Brace Jovanovich College Division, 1988.

de Bono, E. *Atlas of Management Thinking.* London: Penguin Books, 1981.

Dickson, G.C.C. "A Comparison of Attitudes Towards Risk Among Business Managers." *Journal of Occupational Psychology,* 1981, pp. 157-164.

Dietz, T., and Rycroft, R. *The Risk Professionals.* New York: Russell Sage Foundation, 1987.

Dilenschneider, R. L. "Values Are the Means and the End." *New York Times,* Dec. 3, 1989, p. C-3.

Donnelly, R. Interview with the author, 1991.

Doria, J. Interview with the author, 1992.

Drucker, P. *Management: Tasks, Responsibilities, Practices.* New York: HarperCollins, 1974.

Drucker, P. *Innovation and Entrepreneurship.* New York: HarperCollins, 1985.

Dunnaway, T. "Morale Coupons." *Training and Development,* May 1992, p. 11.

Dweck, C. S. "Motivational Processes Affecting Learning." *American Psychologist,* 1986, *41,* 1040-1048.

Dyer, J., and Sarin, R. "Relative Risk Aversion." *Management Science,* 1982, *28*(8), 875-886.

Eigen, L., and Siegel, J. *The Manager's Book of Quotations.* New York: AMACOM, 1989.

Elmer-Dewitt, P. "Time for Some Fuzzy Thinking." *Time,* Sept. 25, 1989, p. 79.

Emerson, R. "Self-Reliance." In R. Emerson, *Essays and Lectures.* Washington, D.C.: Library of America, 1983.

Farley, F. "World of the Type T Personality." *Psychology Today,* May 1986, pp. 46–52.

Feinberg, M., and Levinstein, A. "Transforming Your Employees Through Dynamic Leadership." *Washington Sunday Journal,* Nov. 26, 1984, p. 34.

Feld, A. *Success,* Oct. 1989.

Feldman, S. "Reaching for Success: The Makings of a Corporate Culture." *Computer Currents,* 1986, Mar.-Apr., 18–194.

Fischhoff, B., Slovic, P., and Lichtenstein, S. "Lay Foibles and Expert Fables in Judgment About Risks." *Progress in Resource Management and Environmental Planning,* 1981, *3,* 161–202.

Fischhoff, B., and others. *Acceptable Risk.* Cambridge, England: Cambridge University Press, 1981.

Freeman, F. H. "Issues and Observations: Thinking in Time: The Uses of History for Decision Makers." *Issues and Observations,* Fall 1986.

Freeman, F. H. "Review of *The Leadership Challenge: How to Get Extraordinary Things Done in Organizations* by J. Kouzes and B. Posner. *Issues and Observations,* Winter 1988.

Galagan, P. "Between Two Trapezes." *Training and Development Journal,* 1987, pp. 40–50.

Gall, Adrienne. "You Can Take the Manager Out of the Woods." *Training and Development Journal,* Mar. 8, 1987, pp. 54–58.

Garber, R. Interview with the author, 1992.

Gerstenfeld, A., and Sumiyoshi, K. "The Management of Innovation in Japan—Seven Forces That Make the Difference." *Research Management,* Jan. 1988, pp. 30–34.

Gibson, J. "Choosing the Risks to Take." *Washington Post,* Aug. 27, 1978, p. K-2.

Gilder, G. *The Spirit of Enterprise.* New York: Simon & Schuster, 1984.

Goleman, D. "Great Altruists: Science Ponders Soul of Goodness." *New York Times,* 1985, p. C-1.

Goleman, D. "The Psyche of the Entrepreneur." *New York Times,* Feb. 2, 1986a, pp. 30–32.

Goleman, D. "Tailoring the Plan to the Person: Psychology of Taking Risks." *New York Times Magazine,* Nov. 16, 1986b, pp. 37–38.

Gould, L., and others. *Perceptions of Technological Risks and Benefits.* New York: Russell Sage Foundation, 1988.

Graves, R. "Climbing with Mallory." In D. Reuther and J. Thorn (eds.), *The Armchair Mountaineer.* New York: Doubleday, 1984. (Originally published in *Good-bye to All That.* London: Cassell.)

Green, L. "Fear of Trying." *Esquire,* Sept. 1985, p. 41.

Green, M. "How to Rationalize Your Marketing Risks." *Harvard Business Review,* May-June, 1969, pp. 114–123.

Greenhouse, S. "Dicey Days at McDonnell Douglas." *New York Times,* Feb. 22, 1987, p. C-4.

Grey, R., and Gordon, G. "Risk Taking Managers: Who Gets the Top Jobs?" *Management Review,* 1978, 67(1), 8–13.

Grigsby, D., and Leap, T. "Impact of Risk-Taking Attitudes on Performance Appraisal." *Psychological Reports,* 1982, 51, 1139–1147.

Gunther, M. *The Zurich Axioms.* New York: New American Library, 1985.

Hagebak, B. "The Forgiveness Factor: Taking the Risk Out of Efforts to Integrate Human Services." *Public Administration Review,* Jan./Feb. 1982, pp. 72–76.

Hammond, J., III. "Better Decisions with Performance

Theory." *Harvard Business Review*, Nov./Dec. 1987, pp. 123–141.

Handcock, J., and Teevan, R. "Fear of Failure and Risk-Taking Behavior." *Journal of Personality*, 1964, *32*(2), 200–209.

Handy, C. *The Age of Unreason*. Boston: Harvard Business School Press, 1990.

Hanson, R. "Taking Risks and the Penalties of Playing It Safe." *Administrative Management*, June 1977, pp. 26–72.

Hatfield, J., and Cooper, C. "Risk-Takers of the World." *Management Today*, Nov. 1984, pp. 86–88.

Heller, R. *The Great Executive Dream*. New York: Dell Books, 1972.

Heller, R. *The Decision Makers*. New York: Dutton, 1989.

Henderson, L. Interview with the author, 1992.

Herod, C. Interview with the author, 1992.

Hersh, A. Interview with the author, 1992.

Hertz, D. "Risk Analysis in Capital Investment." *Harvard Business Review*, Sept./Oct. 1979, pp. 169–181.

Hodder, J., and Riggs, H. "Pitfalls in Evaluating Risky Projects." *Harvard Business Review*, Jan./Feb. 1985, pp. 128–135.

Hollister, J. Interview with the author, 1992.

Hornstein, H. A. *Managerial Courage*. New York: Wiley, 1986.

Hunsaker, P. "Incongruity, Adaptation, Capability, and Risk Preference in Turbulent Decision-Making Environment." *Organizational Behavior and Human Performance*, 1975, 14, 173–185.

Hyatt, J. C., and Naj, A. K. "GE Is No Place for Autocrats, Welch Decrees." *Wall Street Journal*, Mar. 3, 1992, p. B-1.

Iacocca, L. "In Order To: Compromise and Competency." Speech delivered at the American Bar Association Annual Convention, Aug. 10, 1987.

Imai, M. *Kaizen: The Key to Japan's Competitive Success.* New York: McGraw-Hill, 1986.

Inaba, S. "Strategic Alliance an Anchor in World Markets." *Manufacturing Week,* Dec. 21, 1987, p. 15.

Irving, R. "Solvitur in Excelsis." In D. Reuther and J. Thorn (eds.), *The Armchair Mountaineer.* New York: Doubleday, 1984. (Originally published in *The Romance of Mountaineering.* 1938.)

Isenberg, D. "The Tactics of Strategic Opportunism." *Harvard Business Review,* Mar./Apr. 1987, pp. 92–97.

Jeffers, S. *Feel the Fear and Do It Anyway.* New York: Fawcett Columbine, 1987.

Jensen, N. "Relationship of Risk-Taking and Other Variables to Women's Career Choices." Unpublished doctoral dissertation, 1981.

Kazantzakis, N. *Zorba the Greek.* (C. Wildman, trans.) New York: Simon & Schuster, 1952.

Keen, P. *Competing in Time: Using Telecommunications for Competitive Advantage.* New York: Ballinger, 1988.

Keen, P. *Shaping the Future.* Boston: Harvard Business School Press, 1991.

Keen, P. Interview with the author, 1991.

Kehrer, D. *Doing Business Boldly: The Art of Taking Intelligent Risks.* New York: Times Books, 1989.

Keyes, R. *Chancing It: Why We Take Risks.* Boston: Little, Brown, 1985.

Kiechel, W., III. "Summoning Managerial Courage." *Fortune,* Jan. 19, 1987, pp. 3–4.

Klemm, R. Interview with the author, 1992.

Kogan, N., and Wallach, M. "Risk Taking as a Function of the Situation, the Person, and the Group." *New Directions in Psychology III.* Troy, Mo.: Holt, Rinehart & Winston, 1967.

Kouzes, J. "When Leadership Collides with Loyalty." *New York Times,* Jan. 24, 1988, p. F-3.

Kuczmarski, T. *Managing New Products.* Englewood Cliffs, N.J.: Prentice-Hall, 1988.

Labich, K. "The Innovators." *Fortune,* June 6, 1988a, pp. 50–64.

Labich, K. "The Seven Keys to Business Leadership." *Fortune,* Oct. 24, 1988b, pp. 58–66.

"Labor Letter: Our Bosses Aren't Very Responsive, Most Workers Believe." *Wall Street Journal,* Oct. 3, 1989, p. 1.

Lee, F., and Bednar, R. "Effects of Group Structure and Risk-Taking Disposition on Group Behavior, Attitudes, and Atmosphere." *Journal of Counseling Psychology,* 1977, 24(3), 191–199.

Lee, T., Fisher, J., and Yau, T. "Getting Things Done: Is Your R&D on Track?" *Harvard Business Review,* Jan./Feb. 1986, pp. 34–44.

Lesher, R. Interview with the author, 1992.

Libby, R., and Fishburn, P. "Behavioral Models of Risk Taking in Business Decisions: A Survey and Evaluation." *Journal of Accounting Research,* Fall 1977, pp. 272–292.

Linden, D. "Dreary Days in the Dismal Science." *Forbes,* Jan. 21, 1991, pp. 68–71.

Lombardo, M. "Brent's World." *Issues and Observations,* 1988, 8(1), 1.

Loomis, C. Review of *Native Stones: A Book About Climbing,* by David Craig. *London Review of Books,* July 9, 1987, pp. 5–6.

Loucks, V., Jr. "A Reclamation of Leadership: Risk and Long Term Investment." *Vital Speeches of the Day,* Feb. 8, 1991, pp. 76–78.

Loughman, M. "The Varieties of Climbing." In D. Reuther and J. Thorn (eds.), *The Armchair Mountaineer.* New York: Charles Scribner's Sons, 1984. (Originally published in Loughman, M. *Learning to Rock Climb.*)

Lupfer, M., and Jones, M. "Risk Taking as a Function of

Skill and Change Orientations." *Psychological Reports*, 1971, *28*, 27–33.

MacCrimmon, K., and Wehrung, D. *Taking Risks: The Management of Uncertainty.* New York: Free Press, 1986.

McDowell, J. "Job Loyalty: Not the Virtue It Seems." *New York Times*, Mar. 3, 1985, p. A-1.

McEwan, B. "The Risk Management Approach to Career Planning." *Supervisory Management*, Jan. 1984, pp. 13–19.

McGinnis, M. "The Key to Strategic Planning: Integrating Analysis and Intuition." *Sloan Management Review*, Fall 1984, pp. 45–52.

Mackenzie, K. "The Effects of Status upon Group Risk Taking." *Organizational Behavior and Human Performance*, 1970, *5*, 517–541.

March, J., and Shapira, Z. "Managerial Perspectives on Risk and Risk Taking." *Management Science*, 1987, *33*(11), 1404–1418.

Marone, N. *Women and Risk: How to Master Your Fears and Do What You Never Thought You Could Do.* New York: St. Martin's Press, 1992.

Marris, P. *Loss and Change.* New York: Pantheon Books, 1974.

Marting, L. Interview with the author, 1993.

Masters, E. L. "George Gray." In *Spoon River Anthology.* New York: Collier, 1969.

May, R. *The Courage to Create.* New York: Bantam Books, 1975.

Meyer, L. "'Can-Do' Can Be Deadly." *Washington Post*, Mar. 3, 1986, p. C-5.

Milburn, T., and Billings, R. "Decision-Making Perspectives from Psychology." *American Behavioral Scientist*, 1976, *20*(1), 111–125.

Miller, J. "States of Synergy." *World Winter*, 1988, pp. 6–7.

Mirabile, R., and others. "Soft Skills, Hard Numbers." *Training,* Aug. 1987, pp. 53–56.

Moore, M., and Gergen, P. "Risk Taking and Organizational Change." *Training and Development Journal,* June 1985, pp. 72–76.

Moore, P. *The Business of Risk.* Cambridge, England: Cambridge University Press, 1983.

Mueller, R. *Risk, Survival, and Power: Axioms Managers Live By.* Washington, D.C.: American Management Association, 1970.

Murphy, S. E., Sperling, J. G., and Murphy, J. D. *The Literature of Work.* Phoenix, Ariz.: University of Phoenix Press, 1991.

Murray, J. "Properly Managed Risk Key to Progress." *Computer World,* Feb. 11, 1985, p. 49.

National Governors' Association. *Report of the Task Force on Research and Technology.* Washington, D.C.: National Governors' Association, 1989.

Nelson, M. "The Things You Do? Make Them New." *Washington Post,* Mar. 11, 1988, p. N-52.

Neuharth, A. *Confessions of an S.O.B.* New York: Doubleday, 1989.

Nord, W. "A Liberal Case for Religion in School." *Washington Post,* July 6, 1986, p. B-1.

Oakes, F. "Taking Human Error Out of the Decisions." *Management Today,* July 1988, pp. 33–41.

Oakes, W.R.T. Interview with the author, 1991.

Olesen, D. "U.S. Lost the Technology Lead, but Producers Are Waking Up." *Manufacturing Week,* Mar. 21, 1988, p. 22.

Orpen, C. "Risk-Taking Attitudes Among Indian, United States, and Japanese Managers." *Journal of Social Psychology,* 1983, *120,* 283–284.

Osborne, D., and Gaebler, T. *Reinventing Government: How the Entrepreneurial Spirit Is Transforming the Public Sector.* Reading, Mass.: Addison-Wesley, 1992.

Patton, G., Jr. "The Effects of Weapons on War." *Infantry Journal,* 1930, *37*(5), 483–488.

Peter, L. *Peter's Quotations: Ideas for Our Time.* New York: Bantam Books, 1979.

Peters, T. "Business in the Future Tense." *Washington Post,* Apr. 10, 1987a, p. C-3.

Peters, T. *Thriving on Chaos: Handbook for a Management Revolution.* New York: Knopf, 1987b.

Pike, R. *Tall Trees, Tough Men.* New York: W. W. Norton, 1967.

"Planning Plan for Emergencies." *Pryor Report,* Sept. 1986, p. 5.

Pollock, M., and Pollock, J. "The Venture Survey: Are You a Risk Taker?" *Venture,* July 1986, p. 24.

Primozic, K., and Leben, J. *Strategic Choices: Supremacy, Survival, or Sayonara.* New York: McGraw-Hill, 1991.

Quick, T. "Expectancy Theory in Five Simple Steps." *Training and Development Journal,* July 1988, pp. 30–32.

Quinn, J. "Technological Innovation, Entrepreneurship, and Strategy." *Sloan Management Review,* Spring 1979, pp. 73–82.

Raddock, D. *Assessing Corporate Political Risk: A Guide for International Businessmen.* Lanham, Md.: Rowman & Littlefield, 1986.

Random House Dictionary of the English Language. (2nd ed.) New York: Random House, 1987.

Rescher, N. *Risk: A Philosophical Introduction to the Theory of Risk Evaluation and Management.* Lanham, Md.: University Press of America, 1983.

"Risk. . . ." *Washington Post,* May 26, 1986, p. A-1.

"Risk Taking: Achievement in Motivation." *Pryor Report,* Aug. 1986, p. 8.

"Risk Taking Toward Innovation." *Training and Development Journal,* Apr. 1987, p. 57.

Ritz Carlton Hotels. *Malcolm Baldrige National Quality Award Application.* 1991.

Rotter, J. "External Control and Internal Control." *Psychology Today,* June 1971, pp. 42–58.

Roussel, P. "Cutting Down the Guesswork and R&D." *Harvard Business Review,* Sep./Oct. 1983, pp. 154–160.

Rowan, R. *The Intuitive Manager.* Boston: Little, Brown, 1986.

Rowe, W. *An Anatomy of Risk.* New York: Wiley, 1977a.

Rowe, W. *What Is Risk?* Melbourne, Fla.: Krieger, 1977b.

Ryan, K. D., and Oestreich, D. K. *Driving Fear Out of the Workplace: How to Overcome the Invisible Barriers to Quality, Productivity, and Innovation.* San Francisco: Jossey-Bass, 1991.

Samuelson, R. "Why Bigness Breeds Waste." *Washington Post,* Oct. 7, 1987, pp. F-1, F-3.

Schlossberg, H. "Employee Empowerment Drives Award-Winning Firms." *Marketing News,* Aug. 19, 1991, p. 6.

Schon, D. "The Fear of Innovation." In R. Hainer, S. Kingsbury, and D. Gleicher (eds.), *Uncertainty in Research Management and New Product Development.* New York: Reinhold, 1967.

Schwartz, J. "NASA's Success Relaxed Vigilance over Reliability of Machines." *Washington Post,* May 26, 1986, p. A-1.

Scollard, J. *Risk to Win: A Woman's Guide to Success.* New York: Macmillan, 1989.

Seibert, D. "Governance Unfettered: Preserving the Right to Risk Failure." *Directors and Boards,* Fall 1987.

"Setbacks: What's the Worst That Can Happen?" *Pryor Report,* Oct. 3, 1985.

Shamlin, T. "The Science of Taking Risks." *Manufacturing Engineering,* June 1989, pp. 65–66.

Siegelman, E. *Personal Risk: Mastering Change in Love and Work.* New York: HarperCollins, 1983.

Silas, C. "Where Have All the Risk Takers Gone?" *Vital Speeches of the Day*, Feb. 21, 1991, pp. 530–533.

Singer, A. "Taking Risks in Business: How Useful Are the Theories?" *Accountancy*, Aug. 1981, pp. 80–84.

Singer, A., and Singer, M. "Risk: Probability or Personality?" *Accountancy*, Aug. 1984, p. 105.

Singh, J. "Performance, Slack and Risk Taking in Organizational Decision Making." *Academy of Management Journal*, 1986, 29(3), 562–585.

Singh, N. "Risk Taking, Achievement Imagery, and Personnel Functions in Entrepreneurship: A Psychological Analysis." *Indian Journal of Psychology*, 1970, 45 121–139.

Sisson, S. "Managerial Risk Taking." *Training and Development Journal*, Jan. 1985, pp. 39–42.

Sisson, S. "Getting Employees to Show Initiative." *Supervisory Management*, Jan. 1986, pp. 17–19.

Skrzycki, C. "A Different Style of Leadership." *Washington Post*, Jan. 13, 1991, p. H-3.

Skrzycki, C., and others. "Risk Takers." *U.S. News and World Report*, Jan. 26, 1987, pp. 60–67.

Slovic, P., Fischhoff, B., and Lichtenstein, S. "Rating the Risks." *Environment*, 1979, 21(3), pp. 14–20, 36–39.

Steele, L. *Managing Technology: The Strategic View.* New York: McGraw-Hill, 1988.

Sterngold, J. "Advice from Japan: It's Not Just Some Cars, It's the Future." *New York Times*, Jan. 12, 1992, pp. D-1.

Stevenson, H., and Gumpert, D. "The Heart of Entrepreneurship." *Harvard Business Review*, Mar./Apr. 1985, pp. 85–94.

Straw, B., and Ross, J. "Knowing When to Pull the Plug." *Harvard Business Review*, Mar./Apr. 1987, pp. 68–74.

Sylvester, K. "Risk and the Culture of Innovation." *Governing*, Oct. 1992, pp. 46–50.

Taylor, C. Interview with the author, 1992.

Thurow, L. *The Zero-Sum Solution: Building a World-*

Class American Economy. New York: Simon & Schuster, 1985.

Toulmin, S., Rieke, R., and Janik, A. *An Introduction to Reasoning.* (2nd ed.) New York: Macmillan, 1984.

Training Director's Forum Newsletter, June/July 1987, p. 6.

Tullar, W., and Johnson, D. "Group Decision-Making and the Risky Shift: A Trans-National Perspective." *International Journal of Psychology,* 1973, 8(2), 117–123.

Tversky, A., and Kahneman, D. "The Framing of Decisions and the Psychology of Choice." *Science,* 1981, *211,* 453–458.

"Unleashing the Risk Takers." *Marketing Communicator,* June 1985, pp. 23–26.

Uris, A. *The Executive Interviewer's Deskbook.* Houston: Gulf, 1978.

Viscott, D. *Risking.* New York: Pocket Books, 1977.

Vlek, C., and Stallen, P. J. "Judging Risks and Benefits in the Small and in the Large." *Organizational Behavior and Human Performance,* 1981, *28,* 235–271.

Vona, C., and Herbich, T. "Battling Global Risk." *Financial Technology Forum,* Dec. 1987, pp. 30–31.

Vroom, V., and Pahl, B. "Relationship Between Age and Risk Taking Among Managers." *Journal of Applied Psychology,* 1971, *55*(5), 399–405.

Wagner, B. "Making the Career Leap!" *Success,* 1989, pp. 38–45.

Waitley, D. *The Joy of Working.* New York: Ballantine Books, 1985.

Waterman, B. "Go with Your Gut." *Success,* June 1988, p. 24.

Webb, M. "New Companies Not Necessarily Risky Business." *Washington Post,* Oct. 16, 1989, p. F-5.

Webber, A. M. "What's So New About the New Economy?" *Harvard Business Review,* Jan.-Feb. 1993, pp. 24–42.

Webber, E., and Bottom, W. "Axiomatic Measures of Perceived Risk: Some Tests and Extensions." *Journal of Behavioral Decision Making,* 1989, 2, 113–131.

Weiss, R. "The Mystery of Why We Take Risks." *Washington Post,* Aug. 23, 1987, p. B-3.

Weiss, W. "Cutting Down the Risks in Decision Making." *Supervisory Management.* May 1985a, pp. 15–16.

Weiss, W. *Decision Making for First Time Managers.* New York: AMACOM, 1985b.

"What Makes People Take Risks?" *Training,* 15.

Wiss, T. Interview with the author, 1993.

Wolf, D. Interview with the author, 1992.

Wriston, W. B. *Risk and Other Four-Letter Words.* New York: Perennial Library, 1986.

Yates, J. F. (ed.). *Risk-Taking Behavior.* New York: Wiley, 1992.

Young, G. "The Measure of Courage." In D. Reuther and J. Thorn (eds.), *The Armchair Mountaineer.* New York: Charles Scribner's Sons, 1984. (Originally published in *Young's Mountain Craft.*)

Zadravec, K. "The Strange Invention Called Hope." *Washington Post,* Dec. 16, 1989, p. F-5.

Zemke, R. "American Heroes: There's Little Bit of Ollie North in Many a CEO's Heart." *Training Directors' Forum Newsletter,* Aug. 1987, p. 7.

Zuckerman, M. *Biological Bases of Sensation Seeking: Impulsivity and Anxiety.* Hillsdale, N.J.: Erlbaum, 1983.

Index

This page constitutes a continuation of the copyright page.

Figure 1.1 (p. 7), Figure 1.2 (p. 9), and Figure 5.1 (p. 95): Reprinted by permission from pages 3, 7, and 24 of *Risk and Insurance* by Athearn, Pritchett, and Schmit. Copyright © 1989 by West Publishing Company. All rights reserved.

Chapter Two epigraph (p. 19): Excerpt from RISK AND OTHER FOUR-LETTER WORDS by Walter B. Wriston. Copyright © 1986 by Walter B. Wriston. Reprinted by permission of HarperCollins Publishers Inc.

Pp. 21–22: Excerpts from "Outplacement Blues." Used by permission of the author.

Pp. 30–31: Discussion of Ritz-Carlton Hotel chain used by permission of Ritz-Carlton.

P. 37: Excerpts from Zorba The Greek by Nikos Kazantzakis. COPYRIGHT © 1953 by Simon & Schuster, Inc. COPYRIGHT RENEWED © 1981 by Simon & Schuster, Inc. Reprinted by permission of Simon & Schuster, Inc.

Pp. 37–38: Lines from "George Gray" from *Spoon River Anthology* by Edgar Lee Masters. Originally published by the Macmillan Co. Permission by Ellen C. Masters.

P. 47: Exercise 3.2. Adapted from Rotter, 1971. Used by permission.

P. 79: Figure 4.1. From THRIVING ON CHAOS by Tom Peters. Copyright © 1987 by Excel, a California Limited Partnership. Reprinted by permission of Alfred A. Knopf, Inc.

Figure 5.2 (p. 98) and Table 5.1 (p. 99): Reprinted with the permission of The Free Press, a Division of Macmillan, Inc. from TAKING RISKS: The Management of Uncertainty by Kenneth R. MacCrimmon and Donald A. Wehrung. Copyright © 1986 by Kenneth R. MacCrimmon and Donald A. Wehrung.

Chapter Ten epigraph (p. 169): Used by permission of Phillips Petroleum Company.